# Adfluence

## Influencing Audiences with Powerful Advertising Strategies

By
Nathan Venture, D

**WELL-BEING**
PUBLISHING

# Adfluence

Influencing Audiences with Powerful
Advertising Strategies

# Contents

# Introduction:
# The Art of Influence in Advertising

Advertising, at its core, is a dance between brands and consumers. This intricate ballet hinges on the art of influence. In today's world, where consumers are inundated with a deluge of messages daily, capturing attention is both a science and an art form. It's no longer just about selling a product; it's about creating a connection and fostering loyalty.

Understanding the mechanics of influence is essential for anyone in the marketing sphere. From the seasoned professional to the budding entrepreneur, mastering this art can be the difference between success and mediocrity. Influence in advertising is not about manipulation; it's about guiding potential customers to see the value in what you're offering. Advertisers must be adept psychologists, storytellers, and strategists all wrapped into one.

Why is influence so crucial? Because humans are not purely rational beings. We are driven by emotions, biases, and subconscious triggers. The best advertising campaigns understand this and tap into those deep-seated elements. This book aims to shed light on these dynamics and equip you with the tools to wield influence responsibly and effectively.

First, let's acknowledge the foundations: human psychology. Our brains are wired in specific ways that influence how we perceive and react to messages. Recognizing these patterns can help you craft ads that resonate on a personal level. Think of it as unlocking the secrets of human behavior to make your campaigns more compelling.

Consider cognitive biases, for example. These are mental shortcuts our brains use to make decisions more efficiently. By understanding biases like confirmation bias or availability heuristic, you can tailor your ads to fit within these frameworks, making them more persuasive.

Equally important are emotional triggers. Emotions can override logic in many decision-making processes. An advertisement that tugs at the heartstrings or invokes a sense of urgency can often outperform one that relies solely on facts and figures. Leveraging emotional appeal can make your brand more relatable and memorable.

Crafting your message is where the art truly comes into play. Clear communication is non-negotiable. A muddled message will get lost amidst the noise. Your headline must be a hook that captures attention instantly. Once you've grabbed the viewer, storytelling keeps them engaged. Stories create a narrative that people can connect with, making your product or service more appealing.

Next up is the visual impact. Humans are visual creatures, and the right design can make all the difference. Your logo and overall design should tell a story about your brand at a glance. Color theory plays a significant role here—choosing the right colors can elicit specific emotional responses and improve brand recognition.

Consistency across platforms ensures that your message and brand identity are coherent, whether consumers encounter you online or offline. It's about creating a seamless experience that reinforces your brand's values and promises.

Speaking of online, the digital advertising revolution has drastically changed the landscape. Social media strategies, SEO, and influencer marketing are now key tools in the advertiser's toolkit. Each platform offers unique opportunities and requires tailored strategies to maximize impact.

However, traditional media is not dead; it has evolved. Integrating traditional and digital campaigns can amplify your reach and effectiveness. Print, radio, and TV still have their place, especially when used in conjunction with new-age digital tactics.

Understanding and segmenting your audience is another pillar of effective advertising. It's about knowing who your customers are, what they want, and how they think. Demographic and psychographic profiling allows for more tailored messaging, ensuring that your ads speak directly to the people most likely to be interested.

To measure success, metrics and analytics are indispensable. Defining key performance indicators (KPIs) helps you track your progress and adjust your strategies. Analysis tools and techniques provide insights into what works and what doesn't, allowing for continuous improvement.

Ethical advertising is about building trust and maintaining transparency. In a world where consumers are more informed and skeptical than ever, honesty and integrity can set your brand apart. Responsibility to consumers is not just a moral obligation; it's a competitive advantage.

Looking to the future, emerging technologies and trends will continue to shape advertising. Staying adaptable and innovative is crucial. The strategies that work today might not be as effective tomorrow, so always be ready to evolve.

Budgeting is another critical aspect. Allocating resources wisely ensures that you get the most out of your advertising spend. It's about finding cost-effective platforms and methods that deliver the best results. Creativity plays a huge role here; often, the most innovative ideas come from working within constraints.

Finally, building a brand through advertising requires a long-term vision. A strong brand identity creates loyalty and trust over time.

Consistent, authentic messaging will help establish a lasting connection with your audience.

The journey to mastering the art of influence in advertising is ongoing and ever-changing. By understanding the principles outlined in this book and applying them with creativity and ethical considerations, you'll be well on your way to creating impactful, lasting campaigns.

# Chapter 1:
## The Power of Persuasion

Effective persuasion lies at the heart of every successful advertising campaign, and its power can't be overstated. It's not just about convincing people to buy a product or service; it's about influencing attitudes, beliefs, and ultimately, behaviors. Understanding the psychological mechanisms behind decision-making can elevate your strategies from good to extraordinary. By tapping into cognitive biases and emotional triggers, you can create messages that resonate deeply and drive action. In this chapter, we'll explore how the art of persuasion can transform your advertising efforts, equipping you with the skills needed to truly connect with your audience and foster lasting relationships. Whether you're looking to increase sales, inspire creativity, or build brand loyalty, mastering the power of persuasion will be your key to success.

## Understanding Human Psychology

Understanding human psychology is at the core of mastering the power of persuasion. To effectively influence consumer behavior, it's essential to grasp how people think, feel, and make decisions. This involves diving deep into concepts like cognitive biases, which can shape and sometimes skew our perceptions and choices. Emotional triggers, on the other hand, tap into the raw, often subconscious feelings that drive actions. By blending an understanding of these psychological intricacies with practical advertising strategies, you can craft messages that resonate on a personal level, fostering stronger connections and driving desired outcomes. This knowledge doesn't just inform your approach—it transforms it, turning a good campaign into a great one by leveraging the very human elements that underlie every decision.

**Cognitive Biases in Decision Making** play an influential role in shaping consumer behavior and, consequently, the success of any advertising campaign. Marketing professionals, business owners, and anyone interested in the field of persuasion need to understand these biases to craft messages that resonate with their target audience. If you're looking to inspire action or drive sales, recognizing and leveraging cognitive biases is essential.

First off, let's clarify what cognitive biases are. They're systematic patterns of deviation from norm or rationality in judgment. Essentially, these are the shortcuts our brains take to make decisions quickly. While these biases can lead to irrational decisions, they are prevalent because they help us cope with the overwhelming amount of information we encounter daily.

One of the most well-known biases is the "Anchoring Bias." This occurs when individuals rely heavily on the first piece of information they receive (the "anchor") when making decisions. Imagine you're selling a product and a consumer sees a "strikethrough" price followed by a discounted one. The initial higher price acts as an anchor, making the discount seem more significant and the offer more appealing.

Another important bias to consider is the "Confirmation Bias." This bias leads people to favor information that confirms their preexisting beliefs while disregarding information that contradicts them. In advertising, this means creating content that resonates with your audience's current beliefs and values. If you can align your message with what your audience already thinks, they are more likely to accept and act on it.

The "Bandwagon Effect" is also crucial. This is a psychological phenomenon where people do something primarily because others are doing it, often ignoring their own beliefs or preferences. The power of social proof—like customer reviews, testimonials, or showing how many others have chosen your product—utilizes the bandwagon effect to influence potential customers. They see a thriving customer base and think, "If others are happy with this, I will be too."

"Scarcity," another bias, is the principle that people assign more value to opportunities that are less available. Limited-time offers, flash sales, and countdown timers can create a sense of urgency, prompting quicker decision-making. The less time or availability perceived, the more valuable the opportunity becomes in the consumer's mind.

"In-group Bias," where people give preferential treatment to others they perceive to be members of their own group, offers a powerful tool for advertisers. You can create marketing campaigns that make the audience feel included in a prestigious "in-group," whether through exclusive clubs, memberships, or insider information.

Then there's the "Loss Aversion Bias." Research shows that the pain of losing is psychologically twice as powerful as the pleasure of gaining. For marketers, framing messages to highlight what the consumer stands to lose rather than what they could gain can be incredibly effective. "Don't miss out on these savings" can be more compelling than "Act now to save."

Another fascinating bias is the "Mere Exposure Effect." This bias suggests that individuals develop a preference for things merely because they are familiar with them. Consistent branding and repeated exposure to your ads can make your brand more likable and trustworthy without the consumer being consciously aware of it.

The "Halo Effect," where an individual's overall impression of something influences their feelings and thoughts about its character, is also important. When a product is associated with a positive image or a well-liked celebrity, the favorable impression extends to the product itself, making it more appealing.

"Authority Bias" and "Trustworthiness" are equally significant. People tend to follow and trust authority figures. When an expert or someone with significant influence endorses your product, it immediately gains credibility and trust. Utilizing endorsements, partnerships, or expert reviews can leverage this bias effectively.

Recognizing these cognitive biases in decision-making helps in creating targeted, efficient, and compelling advertising strategies. However, ethical considerations must be at the forefront. Exploiting these biases to manipulate or deceive can build distrust and damage your brand's reputation. Ethical persuasion prioritizes transparency and respects consumer autonomy, fostering long-term loyalty and trust.

Incorporating an understanding of cognitive biases doesn't mean manipulating your audience; it means speaking their language. Advertising becomes a dialogue where you anticipate how your audience thinks and feels, then craft messages that resonate on a deeper psychological level. This approach not only enhances your campaign's effectiveness but also builds a genuine connection with your consumers.

Ultimately, marketing professionals who harness the power of cognitive biases ethically can craft persuasive, impactful, and memorable campaigns. This knowledge is your toolkit for inspiring action, fostering loyalty, and driving success. Remember, understanding human psychology isn't just about influencing decisions; it's about creating value and building relationships that stand the test of time.

**Emotional Triggers in Consumer Behavior** are a cornerstone in understanding how and why people make purchasing decisions. Emotions act as a powerful driver, often bypassing the rational mind to create an immediate, instinctive reaction. For marketing professionals, it's not just about recognizing these triggers but about strategically integrating them into campaigns to create a genuine connection with the audience. Think of emotions as the catalyst that turns product awareness into genuine desire.

Appealing to emotions isn't a new concept in advertising, but the sophistication of today's campaigns necessitates a deep comprehension of various emotional triggers and their impact on consumer behavior. Different emotions can have radically different effects. Happiness, for instance, is often used to foster brand loyalty. Ads that stimulate joy and contentment can encourage repeat business and long-term customer relationships. Nike's campaigns, often focused on the exhilaration of athletic achievement, leave consumers feeling empowered and ready to purchase.

Fear, on the other hand, is another potent emotional trigger. While it might sound negative, fear-based marketing is effective, particularly in sectors like insurance, health, and security. The idea is to create a sense of urgency and necessity. For example, advertisers for home security systems often highlight the dangers of potential burglaries, compelling consumers to consider the safety of their homes and loved ones.

One must tread carefully with fear, though. Overuse or misuse can backfire and result in consumer alienation. It's a delicate balance to strike—instilling the right amount of concern to provoke action without crossing the line into manipulation or exploitation. But when done ethically and thoughtfully, it can lead to immediate and impactful results. Successful campaigns manage to incite action while still fostering trust and reliability.

Another powerful emotional trigger is a sense of belonging or community. Humans are inherently social creatures who seek acceptance and recognition within groups. Brands that tap into this desire can create intensely loyal customer bases. Apple's advertising often showcases not just the product but the lifestyle and community that comes with being an Apple user. The underlying message is clear: owning an Apple product means you belong to an exclusive, forward-thinking community.

Nostalgia is also an impactful emotional trigger. It taps into a consumer's longing for the past, evoking memories that are often linked to positive emotions. This can be particularly effective with various demographics who may reminisce about different eras. Advertisements that use retro imagery, classic tunes, or references to 'the good old days' can strike an emotional chord that makes the brand more memorable and appealing. Coca-Cola's nostalgic holiday campaigns leverage this trigger masterfully, creating a warm, fuzzy feeling that's intertwined with the brand itself.

Sadness, though seemingly counterintuitive, also has a place in emotional marketing. It can create empathy, shift perceptions, and invite altruistic behavior. Campaigns by non-profit organizations often use this strategy to evoke a sense of compassion and prompt donations or support for a cause. These ads typically tell a story that tugs at the heartstrings, compelling viewers to take action. The emotional impact of such stories stays longer with the audience, creating a lasting impression of the brand's ethos and values.

Surprise and anticipation are other emotions that brands manipulate to their advantage. Surprise can take many forms, such as unexpected humor, plot twists, or reveal campaigns. These elements make an ad more captivating and create buzz around a product. Anticipation, particularly in product launches or pre-release events, builds excitement and a sense of urgency to be among the first to own or experience something new. Tesla's pre-orders for its vehicles often create spikes in consumer interest through carefully managed anticipation and limited availability.

The sensation of power and achievement can also be significant motivators. Ads that highlight personal empowerment, success stories, and the attainment of goals resonate strongly with ambitious, forward-thinking consumers. This sense of empowerment is evident in job search platforms like LinkedIn, which often showcase stories of professional success that inspire users to strive for similar achievements.

Furthermore, the integration of emotional triggers doesn't just bolster consumer interest and engagement; it can significantly impact brand recall and loyalty. Emotions are processed in the brain's limbic system, the same area where memories are created and stored. By linking strong emotions with your product, you make it easier for consumers to remember your brand.

It's also worth noting the increasingly data-driven nature of emotional marketing. With advanced analytics and AI, brands can now better understand what emotional triggers resonate most with their target audience. These insights allow for more precise and effective emotional appeals in advertising, whether through personalized content, tailored messages, or dynamic ad presentations that adjust in real-time based on user reactions.

In conclusion, emotional triggers in consumer behavior are more than just a tool—they're a fundamental aspect of how we interact with brands. By skillfully tapping into the right emotions, advertising can transcend traditional methods, creating not just a purchase but a truly memorable and impactful experience for the consumer. The right emotional appeal can make the difference between a one-time sale and a lifelong brand advocate.

# Chapter 2:
# Crafting Your Message

Welcome to the art of crafting a message that resonates, converts, and sticks with your audience. Communication isn't just about speaking clearly; it's about cutting through the noise and making an impact. Your message must be clear, concise, and compelling, painting a picture that invites your audience to see your vision. This chapter dives into the essentials of creating a potent message, including the art of the headline and the power of storytelling in advertising. You'll learn how to harness emotional triggers and cognitive biases to drive decisions in your favor. It's about knowing your audience inside out, tailoring your message to their needs and desires, and delivering it in a way that feels personal and impactful. A well-crafted message isn't just heard; it's remembered, shared, and acted upon. Let's get started on transforming your communication approach and mastering the art of persuasion.

## The Importance of Clear Communication

Clear communication is the bedrock of any successful advertising campaign. When your message is transparent and straightforward, it cuts through the noise and resonates with your audience. It builds trust, simplifies your value proposition, and allows consumers to quickly grasp the benefits of your product or service. As a marketing professional, you're not just selling a product; you're creating a connection. Ambiguity can be the enemy of marketing success, leading to misconceptions or skepticism. By crafting messages that are easy to understand, you remove barriers to engagement and create a compelling narrative that's hard to ignore. Remember, the clarity of your communication reflects the confidence you have in what you're selling, and that confidence can instill a similar feeling in your prospective customers. So, always aim to be clear, concise, and compelling in every communication touchpoint.

**The Art of the Headline** is an indispensable skill that can make or break any advertising campaign. Headlines are the first impression, the initial hook that either grabs the audience's attention or lets it slip away. In today's saturated market, where consumers are bombarded with countless messages, a well-crafted headline is your opportunity to stand out. It's the front door to your message—if the door doesn't intrigue, no one will step inside.

Think of headlines as the handshake in your first interaction with a potential customer. A strong headline is firm and confident, yet inviting. It sets the tone and piques curiosity, compelling the reader to continue engaging with the content. Without a compelling headline, even the most well-thought-out advertising campaign can fall flat. In just a few words, you have to communicate value, intrigue, and urgency.

So, what makes a headline effective? Firstly, it's clarity. Your audience should immediately understand what they're going to get from engaging further. Clarity doesn't mean boring or overly simplistic; it means being precise and to the point. A clear, targeted headline resonates because it addresses the consumer's direct needs or desires. For example, a headline like "Achieve Your Fitness Goals in Just 4 Weeks" speaks directly to the target audience's aspiration in a clear and concise manner.

In addition to clarity, emotional appeal is a crucial factor. Humans are emotional beings, and headlines that tap into feelings of joy, fear, pride, or curiosity can significantly increase engagement. For instance, consider the headline "Are You Ready to Transform Your Life?" It's simple but evokes an emotional response that pushes the reader to think personally about the message. Emotional triggers are powerful tools in capturing attention and driving action.

Another critical component is the element of curiosity. A good headline should spark intrigue without giving everything away. This creates a 'curiosity gap', a psychological phenomenon where people feel compelled to find out more to satisfy their curiosity. For example, "The Secret to Effortless Weight Loss" invites the reader to discover what that secret might be. It promises valuable information and thus encourages further reading.

Furthermore, urgency and exclusivity can drive immediate action. Phrases like "Limited Time Offer" or "Exclusive Access for Members Only" create a sense of urgency and rarity, pushing the reader to act quickly to avoid missing out. This tactic leverages the fear of missing out (FOMO), a powerful motivator in decision-making processes.

Interestingly, the use of numbers and lists in headlines often increases their effectiveness. Numbers provide structure and a sense of deliverable value. Take "7 Tips to Boost Your Sales Today" as an example. This headline doesn't just promise to help; it quantifies the help, making the content seem more digestible and actionable. Plus, it prepares the reader for a structured and organized read.

Let's not overlook the significance of language and wording. Active language, rather than passive, tends to be more engaging and creates a sense of urgency and dynamism. Words like "discover," "unlock," "achieve," and "boost" are action-driven and imply immediate benefits. Conversely, passive language can feel sluggish and less compelling.

Moreover, the inconsistency of headline patterns keeps your audience on their toes. While using proven formulas (like lists or questions) is effective, breaking the mold now and then can be equally impactful.

A headline that surprises—because it breaks conventional rules—can catch the eye precisely for its uniqueness.

It's also important to test your headlines. A/B testing, where you run two different headlines for the same content, can provide invaluable insights into what resonates best with your audience. This practice allows you to refine and perfect your headline strategy continuously. Utilizing analytics to gauge the performance of different headlines will help you understand your audience better and identify what drives higher engagement.

Besides testing, studying successful headlines can be enlightening. Look at campaigns that have gained substantial traction and dissect their headlines. What language did they use? What emotions did they tap into? How did they promise value? Analyzing these factors will enable you to incorporate winning elements into your own headlines.

Furthermore, context is key. Your headline should align with the platform and medium through which your advertisement is delivered. A social media headline might need to be more concise and punchy compared to a headline in an email campaign, where you might have slightly more room to be descriptive. Tailoring your headline to fit the medium ensures maximum impact.

One must also be mindful of honesty and ethical implications. While it's tempting to craft sensational headlines to grab attention, ensuring that your headlines reflect the true content and value of your message is crucial. Misleading headlines can lead to a lack of trust and damage your brand in the long run. Ethics in advertising not only build long-term customer loyalty but also fortify your brand's reputation.

Ultimately, the art of the headline is an ongoing balancing act. You have seconds to make an impression, so each word must count. Clarity, emotion, curiosity, urgency, and ethical practices—all these elements must intertwine seamlessly to create a headline that doesn't just capture attention but also converts it into action. Mastering this art requires both creativity and strategy, but the payoff is worth the effort. When executed well, a headline can be the linchpin of a successful advertising campaign, paving the way for deeper engagement and conversion.

The art of crafting a headline is akin to setting the stage for a performance. The headline is your opening act; get it right, and the audience is primed and ready. Marketing professionals, business owners, and advertisers should invest time and thought into crafting headlines, understanding that this small element can yield immense results. So, the next time you sit down to brainstorm a headline, remember: it's not just a few words at the top of your page; it's the gateway to your audience's heart and mind.

**Storytelling in Advertising** is an art form that goes beyond listing product features or hammering home a call to action. Effective advertising weaves narratives that captivate, engage, and ultimately persuade. While a great story has the power to entertain, it also fulfills a crucial role in embedding a brand's message into the consumer's mind. But what makes storytelling so impactful in the context of advertising? The answer lies in its ability to connect emotionally with the audience.

When you think of advertising, the first thing that might come to mind is a catchy jingle or a memorable slogan. These elements are indeed important, but what gives them staying power is the story behind them. A well-crafted narrative can make a brand more relatable, allowing consumers to see themselves using the product. This ability to see themselves in the story makes the entire message more personal and impactful.

Consider some of the most memorable ad campaigns in history. Coca-Cola's "Share a Coke," for instance, didn't just sell soda; it sold the idea of connection and shared moments. Nike's "Just Do It" isn't just about shoes; it's about overcoming obstacles and pushing limits. These campaigns utilized storytelling to transform mundane products into symbols of broader human experiences.

At its core, storytelling in advertising is about creating a narrative arc that draws people in. This often follows the classic structure: a beginning that sets the stage, a middle that introduces a conflict or challenge, and an end that provides resolution. The protagonist in these stories could be an individual overcoming a struggle with the help of a product, a community coming together through a shared experience, or even the brand itself acting as a hero.

But not all stories are created equal. To be effective, a story must resonate deeply with its intended audience. And this is where understanding your market becomes critical. Knowing the values, aspirations, and pain points of your target audience allows you to craft narratives that hit home. If you're marketing to young professionals, for example, a story about balancing work and life while achieving personal goals might be compelling. On the other hand, if your audience is young parents, a story centered around the joy and challenges of raising children might resonate more deeply.

Emotion drives action, and stories are a powerful way to stir emotions. Whether it's joy, empathy, fear, or excitement, advertisers who master the art of storytelling understand how to evoke the right feelings at the right moments. Emotional triggers can create a lasting impression much deeper than mere rational arguments. For instance, a commercial about a life-saving medical device might not focus solely on its features. Instead, it might tell the story of a family whose lives were changed because of that device, touching on the emotions of relief and gratitude.

Narratives also offer a way to differentiate a brand in a cluttered market. When multiple companies offer similar products or services, how do you stand out? Through storytelling, you can infuse your brand with unique traits and values that set it apart. Take Apple, for example. Much of its advertising is focused not on product specifications but on stories of creativity and innovation. This storytelling approach has helped carve out a unique space in consumers' minds where Apple is seen as a leader in driving change and fostering creativity.

Moreover, stories have the power to build a sense of community and shared identity among consumers. The narratives you develop can help customers feel like they are part of something bigger than themselves. This sense of belonging can be a potent motivator for brand loyalty. Harley-Davidson is a great example of this. Their advertisements are less about the nuts and bolts of their motorcycles and more about the freedom, brotherhood, and rebellious spirit that riding represents. As a result, Harley-Davidson enthusiasts often see themselves as part of a close-knit community united by common values.

Let's not forget about the different mediums through which stories can be told. While traditional media such as TV and print have been staple outlets for storytelling, the digital revolution has opened up new avenues. Social media platforms, blogs, podcasts, and video channels have democratized storytelling, allowing brands to communicate more interactively and collaboratively with their audiences. Each medium offers unique opportunities and challenges, but the fundamental principles of good storytelling remain the same. The key is to understand the strengths of each platform and tailor your story accordingly.

Another essential aspect of storytelling in advertising is authenticity. Consumers today are savvy and can easily spot insincerity. Authentic stories that reflect true-to-life experiences and genuine emotions tend to resonate more. This authenticity builds trust, an invaluable asset in the modern marketplace. Patagonia, for example, is a brand that has used authentic storytelling to build a loyal customer base. Their commitment to environmental sustainability isn't just a marketing gimmick; it's a core part of their brand narrative, reinforced consistently through genuine stories and actions.

It's not just about telling a story, but about creating an experience. Interactive storytelling, where consumers can engage with the narrative, adds a layer of involvement and makes the experience more memorable. Virtual reality (VR) and augmented reality (AR) offer immersive storytelling options that can transport consumers into different worlds and scenarios, making the narrative even more compelling and engaging.

While crafting an engaging story is vital, so too is knowing when and where to deploy it. Context matters just as much as content. The same story might be told differently depending on whether it's displayed on a billboard versus shared as a viral video on social media. Timing, audience demographics, and current trends all play a role in optimizing the impact of your storytelling efforts.

Furthermore, data can be incredibly beneficial in refining your storytelling strategies. Analytics provide insights into what is working and what isn't, allowing you to adjust your narratives for maximum effectiveness. Understanding consumer behavior through data helps in crafting stories that are not only emotionally engaging but also strategically sound. Tools like A/B testing can reveal what types of stories resonate best with different segments of your audience, enabling you to fine-tune your messaging.

Crafting a compelling story requires creativity, but it also demands discipline and strategic thinking. It starts with a deep understanding of your brand's identity, values, and broader mission. Then, you need to align this understanding with consumer insights to create stories that not only engage but also drive action. The most effective stories are those that blend creativity with a clear purpose, addressing both emotional and rational aspects of the consumer's experience.

In conclusion, storytelling in advertising is a multifaceted approach that combines art and science. It's about more than just selling a product—it's about conveying a message that resonates on an emotional level, creating a lasting impression that can turn one-time customers into lifelong brand advocates. Through compelling narratives, brands can build deeper connections with their audience, differentiate themselves in a crowded marketplace, and ultimately drive sustained success. By mastering the art of storytelling, advertisers can leverage this powerful tool to inspire, engage, and convert their audiences, achieving greater impact and lasting influence in the world of marketing.

# Chapter 3:
# Visual Impact and Branding

Visual impact and branding lie at the heart of any successful marketing campaign. An engaging visual presence not only captures attention but also fosters an immediate connection between the consumer and the brand. The right combination of colors, typography, and design elements creates an emotional response that can enhance brand recognition and loyalty. It's essential to maintain consistency in visual elements across all platforms to build a cohesive brand image that resonates with your audience. By crafting visually appealing and strategically designed content, you empower your brand to leave a lasting impression, ensuring it stands out in a crowded marketplace.

## Logo and Design Psychology

Understanding the psychology behind logo and design is crucial in creating a lasting visual impact for your brand. A well-crafted logo isn't just an aesthetic element—it's a powerful tool that communicates your brand's essence at a glance. The right design can evoke emotions, build trust, and establish credibility, making your brand unforgettable in the minds of consumers. By leveraging color, shape, and typography, you can craft a logo that resonates deeply with your target audience. Remember, every design choice sends a message, so be strategic and intentional. A thoughtfully designed logo can serve as the cornerstone of your brand identity, driving recognition and loyalty across all touchpoints.

**Color Theory and Brand Recognition** is essential to understanding how consumers perceive and connect with brands. When we dive into color theory, we're exploring more than just wavelengths and pigments; we're delving into a complex psychological landscape. Colors are a vital part of non-verbal communication, saturating our perceptions and influencing decision-making processes without us even realizing it.

Across all cultures, colors evoke specific emotions and reactions. For instance, red universally signifies urgency and passion, often used in clearance sales to create a sense of urgency. In contrast, blue is associated with trust and dependability, explaining its prevalence in financial sector branding. Understanding these emotional triggers is fundamental to effective brand recognition and resonance.

Consider the golden arches of McDonald's. The choice of red and yellow isn't accidental. Red triggers excitement and appetite, while yellow is associated with happiness and energy. Together, they create a sense of immediate accessibility and pleasure, driving consumer behavior in subtle but powerful ways. This is color theory in action.

Let's talk about how a brand can strategically employ color to stand out in a crowded market. Think of your brand's color palette as a visual identity that communicates your values and promises. Consistency is key here. If your logo, website, and product packaging utilize a coherent color scheme, it strengthens the overall brand image. Consistent use of color builds brand recognition, as repeated exposure causes consumers to make immediate associations with your brand.

It's not just about picking colors that look good together; it's about ensuring that these colors align with your brand's message and target audience's expectations. A luxury brand might use blacks, golds, and silvers to evoke elegance and exclusivity. On the other hand, a brand targeting children would likely use bright, primary colors that speak of fun and energy.

Science backs this up. Studies have shown that color can improve brand recognition by up to 80%. Consumers are also more likely to remember visual details than textual ones. This makes color a powerful tool in leaving a lasting impression. When a brand gets its colors right, it can create strong emotional connections, making the brand unforgettable.

Think of Tiffany & Co. What comes to mind? That distinctive robin's egg blue box doesn't need a logo to be recognized. This specific shade, known as Tiffany Blue, has become synonymous with luxury and exclusivity. By owning a color, a brand creates an enigmatic distinction that can't be easily replicated.

The role of color in brand recognition extends to digital interfaces, too. When users navigate through a website or mobile app, the color scheme affects their experience. Warm colors might stimulate engagement and excitement, while cooler tones could foster a sense of calm and trust. By aligning the digital user experience with the brand's visual identity, companies enhance their overall brand coherence.

Moreover, the implications of color choices go beyond mere aesthetics to encompass issues of accessibility. Brands must be conscious of color blindness and other visual impairments when designing their collateral. Using high contrast and multiple indicators beyond color, such as text or icons, ensures that the brand message is accessible to everyone.

Another fascinating aspect of color theory in branding involves cultural perceptions. For example, white symbolizes purity and cleanliness in Western cultures but can signify mourning in some Eastern cultures. A global brand must take into account these cultural nuances to avoid misinterpretation and to resonate effectively with diverse audiences.

It is also worth noting that trends can influence color perceptions. Colors that might seem bold and cutting-edge now could be seen as outdated in a few years. Staying attuned to color trends while maintaining brand consistency can be a delicate balance, but it's necessary for long-term brand vitality.

Additionally, the saturation and brightness of colors play an important role. Vivid and highly saturated colors are usually eye-catching and can be used to grab attention quickly. In contrast, softer, muted tones may convey sophistication and subtleness. Knowing when and where to utilize different shades and tones can give your brand the edge in different contexts, whether it's a high-energy commercial or a serene product brochure.

Lastly, testing and data analysis play a crucial role in honing your brand's color strategy. Running A/B tests on different color combinations in ads and marketing materials can provide insights into what resonates most with your target audience. Data-driven decisions ensure that your color choices aren't just based on intuition but backed by tangible evidence.

In conclusion, color theory is not just an artistic endeavor but a powerful scientific tool in the arsenal of branding and marketing. By understanding the psychological, cultural, and emotional connotations of colors, brands can craft a visual identity that resonates deeply, stands out in a crowded marketplace, and builds lasting recognition. Consistent, strategic use of color is a linchpin for creating strong, memorable connections with consumers—and in an era where attention is a scarce commodity, these connections are more valuable than ever.

**Consistency Across Platforms** is crucial in today's fragmented media landscape. With so many channels available—social media, email, print, TV, digital ads—the need for a unified brand message has never been more important. Imagine if Coca-Cola's messaging varied wildly between their Instagram posts and their TV commercials; the disconnect would confuse consumers and dilute the brand's impact. The same principle applies to businesses of all sizes. Ensuring consistency across platforms can help you build a cohesive, powerful brand that resonates with your target audience.

Start by establishing clear brand guidelines. These should include everything from your brand's tone and voice to the color schemes and logos you'll use. Consistent use of these elements helps to create a recognizable and trustworthy brand. When consumers encounter a familiar look and feel, whether in a Facebook ad or a LinkedIn post, it reinforces your brand identity and builds trust. This trust, in turn, can increase customer loyalty and drive conversions.

Consistency isn't just about aesthetics; it's also about the core message. Your brand's values, mission, and Unique Selling Proposition (USP) should remain constant across all platforms. If your online content emphasizes eco-friendliness, but your print ads don't mention it, you'll create confusion. To avoid this, keep your key messages front and center, regardless of where you're communicating. This unified messaging strengthens your brand's position and makes it easier for consumers to understand what you stand for.

Another important aspect is adapting your content to fit different platforms while maintaining a consistent message. This can be challenging but is essential for effective communication. Each platform has its nuances—Facebook favors different formats than Twitter, and LinkedIn operates differently from Instagram. Tailor your content to each medium but ensure that the core message and visual elements remain consistent. In other words, the content format may change, but the essence of your brand should not.

Utilize a brand management tool for this. Tools like Canva, Hootsuite, or even more specialized software can help in maintaining a consistent look and feel across various platforms. These tools often come with templates and style guides that ensure every piece of content aligns with your brand guidelines. They also enable teams to collaborate more efficiently, ensuring that everyone is on the same page.

Now, let's talk about the role of training and internal communication in maintaining consistency. Your entire team, from marketing to customer service, needs to understand and embody your brand values and messaging. Conduct regular training sessions to keep everyone aligned. The more your team understands the brand, the easier it is to maintain that consistency when communicating externally. Internal newsletters, regular update meetings, and using a shared brand style guide can go a long way in achieving this.

Consistency across platforms also enhances the customer experience. Imagine a customer encountering your brand on multiple platforms, from a Facebook ad to your website and even a promotional email. If the messaging and design are coherent, the experience is seamless and professional, enhancing the overall brand perception. On the flip side, inconsistent messaging can make the experience jarring and confusing, potentially costing you business.

Remember, brand consistency isn't stagnant—it evolves with your brand. Periodically review your guidelines and make updates to reflect changes in your business or market conditions. If you're introducing a new product line or entering a new market, ensure these changes are reflected consistently across all platforms. Your consumers should never be left guessing about your brand's direction and values.

Testing and feedback are also crucial for maintaining consistency. A/B testing different messages and design elements on various platforms can provide valuable insights into what works best. Use these insights to refine your strategy. Moreover, open channels for customer feedback can help you identify gaps in your consistency. Immediate action on this feedback can help in closing those gaps quickly.

In conclusion, **Consistency Across Platforms** is not just a buzzword but a fundamental aspect of modern brand management. From establishing clear guidelines to tailoring content appropriately for different platforms, every step plays a crucial role in building and maintaining a strong, unified brand. In an age where consumers interact with brands across multiple touchpoints, a consistent branding approach can distinguish you from the competition and build lasting customer relationships.

Consistency doesn't just happen; it's a deliberate, ongoing effort. Employ the right tools, train your team, and continually seek feedback to ensure that your brand message remains powerful and clear, no matter where it's encountered. The result is a cohesive brand presence that not only attracts but retains loyal customers, driving long-term success.

# Chapter 4:
# The Digital Advertising Revolution

The advent of digital advertising has fundamentally reshaped the landscape of marketing, propelling businesses into an era where audience reach, engagement, and conversion can be optimized like never before. With the rise of social media platforms, search engine optimization (SEO), and content marketing strategies, marketers now have unprecedented tools to amplify their brand's message and connect with consumers on a personal level. Digital advertising empowers brands to leverage influencers who resonate with their target audience, creating authentic and influential partnerships that drive engagement. It's about understanding the intricacies of the digital ecosystem and harnessing its power to craft campaigns that are not only effective but also ethically sound. As businesses navigate this revolution, the focus must be on creating value-driven content that resonates with consumers, building trust and fostering long-term loyalty while adapting to the ever-changing digital landscape. This chapter will delve into the strategies and innovations that define modern digital advertising, equipping you with the insights needed to thrive in this dynamic environment.

## Social Media Strategies

The digital advertising landscape has been utterly transformed by the rise of social media, necessitating a strategic approach that deftly balances creativity and data-driven decision-making. For businesses aiming to build brand awareness and foster genuine connectivity with audiences, leveraging platforms like Facebook, Instagram, Twitter,

LinkedIn, and TikTok is essential. This requires not just participation, but a deep understanding of each platform's unique ecosystem—what works on Instagram might not resonate on LinkedIn. Effective social media strategies prioritize authentic engagement, harness powerful visuals, and incorporate customer feedback to continuously refine the approach. By mastering the art of targeted content, storytelling, and timing, marketing professionals can create a resonant brand presence that drives both loyalty and conversion. The constant evolution of these platforms means staying updated on trends and being adaptable, ensuring that strategies remain relevant and impactful in a dynamic digital world.

**SEO and Content Marketing** represents a significant intersection in the evolution of digital advertising. In an age where information is at everyone's fingertips, SEO and content marketing serve as twin pillars supporting a brand's presence online. The art and science of SEO (Search Engine Optimization) involves tailoring content in a manner that attracts search engines, making it easier for potential customers to find your services. But more than just technical adjustments, it's about creating valuable content that genuinely addresses the needs, queries, and desires of your target audience.

When we talk about SEO, we're diving into a multi-faceted strategy. At its core, SEO is about aligning your digital assets—websites, blogs, social media pages—with the algorithms that search engines use to rank content. Keywords, backlinks, and meta descriptions are the old guard of SEO, but the best practices have evolved considerably. Today, search engines like Google prioritize user experience, favoring content that is engaging, authoritative, and genuinely useful. To excel in SEO, one must understand these dynamic criteria and continually adapt.

Consider keyword research as the first step. While it may sound elementary, uncovering which words and phrases your potential customers use to search for your products or services is foundational. Tools like Google Keyword Planner, Ahrefs, and SEMrush can facilitate this process. Once you're equipped with this data, integrating these keywords naturally into your content is crucial. Overstuffing your content with keywords can result in penalization, so the focus should always be on maintaining a natural and fluid reading experience.

But keywords are just the tip of the iceberg. Quality content is the driving force behind effective SEO. This brings us to content marketing. The marriage between SEO and content marketing is one of necessity and synergy. Think of content marketing as the means through which you provide value to your audience—blog posts, articles, videos, infographics—all designed to engage, inform, and convert. High-quality, relevant content not only helps in ranking higher on search engines but also builds trust and authority in your niche.

When executed well, content marketing serves multiple purposes. It captures the attention of potential clients and nurtures existing customer relationships by continually offering value. Take blog posts, for instance. They can serve to answer common queries that your audience has, establish your business as a thought leader in your industry, and drive organic traffic through search engines. Blogs can also be a vehicle for storytelling—an invaluable tool in making an emotional connection with your audience.

Incorporating a coherent content marketing strategy involves planning and consistency. An editorial calendar can help keep your efforts organized and ensure you're regularly providing fresh content. It's not just about quantity but quality, regularity, and relevance. Aligning your content with the interests, problems, and aspirations of your audience can result in prolonged engagement and loyalty.

Moreover, different formats cater to different preferences and consumption patterns. For some, video content on platforms like YouTube or Vimeo might be more engaging than a lengthy article.

Others might prefer podcasts that they can listen to on the go. And let's not forget about social media. Sharing snippets or insights from your blogs and videos on platforms like LinkedIn, Facebook, and Instagram can amplify your reach exponentially.

Social signals—likes, shares, comments—are increasingly factored into search engine algorithms. As your content is shared more widely and engages more users, it naturally begins to rank higher in search engine results. This creates a virtuous cycle where good content attracts engagement, which in turn improves SEO, which then drives more traffic to your content.

Backlinking remains a pivotal aspect of SEO, and content marketing can play a big role here. When other authoritative websites link back to your content, search engines interpret this as a sign of credibility and relevance. This can significantly boost your search rankings. The key is to create content worth linking to. Comprehensive guides, original research, and in-depth articles are more likely to earn these valuable backlinks.

Let's not overlook the importance of local SEO, especially for businesses that operate in specific geographic locations. Optimizing your content with local keywords and registering your business with Google My Business can work wonders in attracting local traffic. Local SEO often involves creating content that is tailored to local interests and news, helping your business become part of the community's digital ecosystem.

User experience (UX) factors into SEO as well. A website's layout, loading speed, mobile-friendliness, and ease of navigation all influence how search engines rank it. Therefore, while content is king, design must also serve to enhance the user experience. A well-designed website supports your content marketing efforts by making it easy for users to find and engage with your content.

The convergence of SEO and content marketing is a dynamic interplay of art and science. The goal is simple: to reach the right people at the right time with the right message. As search engines become more sophisticated, the methods to optimize content will continue to evolve. However, the fundamentals remain constant: user-focused, valuable content coupled with a thorough understanding of SEO principles. By mastering these, you lay a robust foundation for a powerful digital presence that drives traffic, engagement, and ultimately, conversions.

In conclusion, the harmony between SEO and content marketing isn't just a tactical advantage; it's essential for any modern advertising plan. This integrated approach ensures that you're not only visible to your target audience but also building enduring relationships with them. Done right, it turns potential clicks into loyal customers and ephemeral engagements into lasting bonds.

**Leveraging Influencers** in the current digital landscape is more than just a trend—it's a transformative way to connect with audiences in a relatable and authentic manner. As marketing professionals, some of you may already be familiar with influencer marketing, but it's vital to understand the strategic nuances that can turn a good campaign into a game-changing one.

Influencers, with their dedicated followings, have the unique power to build trust and loyalty that brands might struggle to achieve through direct channels. Their followers view them as authorities or trusted friends, making their endorsements much more impactful. Leveraging this dynamic can drive significant traffic, conversion rates, and brand affinity.

First and foremost, it's essential to identify influencers who align with your brand's values and message. They should resonate with your target audience in a way that's natural and genuine. This means looking beyond mere follower counts and focusing on engagement rates and audience demographics. A micro-influencer with 10,000 engaged followers can sometimes offer better ROI than a celebrity with millions of passive followers.

Once you have identified potential influencers, the next step is building a collaborative relationship. This should be a partnership rather than a transactional deal. Allow influencers creative freedom to present your brand in a way that feels authentic to their personal brand. This approach helps maintain their credibility while integrating your product or service seamlessly into their content.

Moreover, integrating influencers into your overall marketing strategy can amplify your campaigns across various channels. It's not just about one-off posts; think long-term relationships and multi-channel campaigns. For instance, an influencer's blog post can be complemented with social media shoutouts, video content, and inclusion in email newsletters. By doing this, you create a cohesive narrative that can be shared across different platforms.

In terms of content, flexibility is key. Influencer-generated content can range from video reviews and unboxings to in-depth tutorials and lifestyle photos. The type of content should align with your campaign objectives and the influencer's strengths. Authenticity is paramount; audiences today are savvy and can easily spot contrived endorsements.

To ensure that your influencer partnerships deliver value, set clear goals and KPIs from the outset. These can include engagement metrics, website traffic, sales conversions, or even social sentiment analysis. Tracking these metrics helps you understand what's working and allows you to optimize future campaigns.

Remember, leveraging influencers isn't just for B2C brands. B2B companies can also benefit significantly from influencer collaborations. Industry experts, thought leaders, and niche content creators can lend credibility to your brand and help you reach specific professional audiences. The principles remain the same: align values, foster genuine relationships, and measure impact.

One of the often-overlooked benefits of influencer marketing is the opportunity for content repurposing. Influencer content can be reused across your brand's own social media channels, websites, and other marketing materials. This not only amplifies the message but also adds a layer of authenticity to your brand voice.

Let's also not forget the legal and ethical considerations. Disclosure and transparency are non-negotiable. The FTC requires influencers to clearly indicate when a post is sponsored. Failing to do so can not only result in legal repercussions but also damage your brand's reputation. Being upfront about your partnerships builds trust with the audience, which is ultimately the foundation of successful influencer marketing.

As you build your influencer strategy, pay attention to evolving trends and platforms. Influencer marketing on emerging platforms like TikTok or Clubhouse may require different approaches compared to more established platforms like Instagram or YouTube. Each platform has its own ecosystem, and understanding these nuances can give you a competitive edge.

Leveraging influencers effectively can set your brand apart in a crowded marketplace. By selecting the right partners, fostering genuine relationships, and integrating influencer content into a cohesive strategy, you'll not only enhance your brand's visibility but also create authentic connections with your audience. Keep iterating, remain flexible, and never underestimate the power of a well-executed influencer campaign.

# Chapter 5:
# Traditional Media and Its Evolution

Traditional media—print, radio, and TV—have undergone significant changes, yet remain pivotal in the advertising landscape. While digital platforms have surged in popularity, the credibility and broad reach of traditional media continue to hold value. The evolution of these channels has been marked by the integration of advanced analytics, enabling more targeted and effective campaigns. Furthermore, savvy marketers are increasingly blending traditional and digital strategies to create cohesive, multi-channel campaigns that leverage the strengths of both worlds. As you navigate this evolving media terrain, understanding how to harness the continued relevance of traditional media while adapting to its modern iterations will be crucial to your success in crafting compelling and impactful advertisements.

## Print, Radio, and TV in the Modern Age

As marketing professionals, you already know that traditional media remains a cornerstone in the advertising landscape. Print, radio, and TV have not become obsolete; rather, they have evolved and adapted to the digital age. Newspapers and magazines now offer online versions and digital subscriptions, extending their reach beyond physical boundaries. Meanwhile, radio has transformed through podcasts and satellite broadcasts, providing on-demand content that meets modern consumer preferences. TV, with the rise of streaming services, has seen a surge in targeted advertising opportunities, ensuring that your message gets in front of the right audience. Understanding how to leverage these traditional platforms in today's digital world allows you to create more comprehensive and impactful campaigns. This blend of old and new media strategies is crucial for building robust brand awareness and engaging a diverse customer base in a dynamic market.

**Integrating Traditional and Digital Campaigns** might sound like a complex puzzle, but when done right, it's a surefire way to amplify your advertising impact. The goal is to blend the strengths of both traditional and digital platforms to create a cohesive, omnichannel experience that resonates with your audience. Picture this: a well-executed print ad that directs consumers to a precisely targeted digital campaign. This isn't just synergy; it's amplification, extension, and evolution of the message across multiple touchpoints.

First, let's talk about consistency. Whether it's a print ad in a magazine or a banner ad on a website, your branding, messaging, and visual elements must be consistent. This uniformity builds trust and reinforces your brand identity. Consumers should be able to recognize your brand no matter where they encounter it. Logo, color scheme, typography, and tone of voice should all be aligned. Think of each element of your campaign as a brushstroke in a larger painting. Consistency in these strokes will create a masterpiece that is both identifiable and memorable.

One powerful strategy is to use traditional media to drive traffic to digital platforms. Say you have a compelling TV commercial airing. Adding a call-to-action (CTA) that prompts viewers to visit your website or follow you on social media can seamlessly bridge the gap between old and new media. A QR code on a print ad can work wonders when it comes to propelling readers into the digital realm instantly. These small yet significant integrations ensure that each piece of the campaign contributes to the overall marketing goals.

The art of storytelling is another crucial factor. Traditional media has a wide reach and is perfect for telling your brand story in a dramatic, emotional fashion. This can generate initial interest and build an emotional connection. Meanwhile, digital platforms offer the opportunity to delve deeper into your story, providing detailed content, interactive experiences, and personalized messaging. The narrative should transition smoothly between platforms, enriching the consumer's journey with consistent and complementary storytelling.

Measurement and adaptability are your best friends in the era of integrated campaigns. Traditional media often poses challenges when it comes to measuring impact. However, integrating digital elements allows for real-time analytics and performance tracking. Utilizing tracking URLs, promotional codes, or specific landing pages, you can gauge the effectiveness of your traditional ads and fine-tune your approach. This dynamic data-driven adaptability means that you can steer your campaign for optimal results, ensuring that both traditional and digital aspects are functioning in harmony.

Simplicity is key. Keep your messages straightforward but impactful. When integrating the two mediums, avoid overwhelming your audience with too much information. Instead, focus on concise, clear, and compelling communication. Traditional media should pique interest and drive the audience towards your digital platform, where they can find more detailed information. Simpler messages in traditional spots can make the audience curious, inviting them to explore further online. This journey from curiosity to engagement is what closes the loop efficiently.

Engaging visual elements can't be stressed enough. Traditional media like billboards, newspapers, or TV rely heavily on visual appeal. Translating these elements cohesively into digital formats can significantly bolster brand recall and recognition. Use high-quality images, videos, and consistent design elements across both mediums to create a seamless visual experience that's hard to ignore. Interactive elements in digital media, such as clickable videos or dynamic ads, can elevate these visuals further and keep the audience engaged longer.

Additionally, consider leveraging demographic data intelligently. Traditional media often targets a broad audience, but digital platforms give the ability to retarget specific demographics with highly tailored messages. Suppose your billboard campaign spans a diverse geographic area. Through demographic data and digital tools, you can identify which segments interacted with your campaign and follow up with personalized online ads. This ensures that no potential lead slips through the cracks and enhances conversion rates.

Innovation should be at the heart of your campaign integration strategy. Augmented Reality (AR) and Virtual Reality (VR) are perfect examples of how traditional and digital media can intersect to create immersive experiences. Imagine a magazine ad that comes to life through AR or a VR experience marketed via a TV commercial. Such innovative integrations can create buzz and deeply engage consumers, providing them with experiences that are both memorable and shareable.

One final aspect to consider is collaboration. Often, the teams working on traditional and digital campaigns might operate in silos. To integrate these campaigns effectively, collaboration between departments is crucial. Regular brainstorming sessions, combined meetings, and a unified strategy can pave the way for cohesive campaigns. Get everyone on the same page with a shared vision and goals that align both traditional and digital efforts. Collaboration leads to creativity, and creativity leads to innovative, integrated campaigns.

In conclusion, **integrating traditional and digital campaigns** isn't just about blending old and new; it's about creating a seamless, multi-platform experience that engages, informs, and converts. It's about harmonizing your message across different mediums, utilizing the strengths of each to create a comprehensive and effective advertising strategy. With consistency, storytelling, measurement, simplicity, visual appeal, demographic targeting, innovation, and collaboration, you can master the art of integrated campaigns and achieve unprecedented success. For marketing professionals and business owners, this approach isn't just beneficial—it's essential.

# Chapter 6:
# Understanding and Segmenting
# Your Audience

Gaining a comprehensive understanding of your audience is the cornerstone of any successful advertising campaign. It's not just about knowing who your customers are; it's about diving deeper into their demographic and psychographic profiles to uncover what makes them tick. Segmenting your audience enables you to create tailored messages that resonate on a personal level, increasing engagement and driving conversion. By identifying niche markets and understanding the unique needs and desires of different audience segments, you can craft highly effective and targeted campaigns. This approach allows you to speak directly to your customers' hearts and minds, ultimately fostering stronger connections and building lasting brand loyalty.

## Demographic and Psychographic Profiling

Understanding and segmenting your audience begins with a deep dive into demographic and psychographic profiling. Demographic profiling involves examining quantifiable characteristics like age, gender, income level, education, and geographical location to identify the general traits of your audience. Psychographic profiling, on the other hand, digs deeper into the psychology of your consumers, exploring their lifestyles, values, interests, and personalities. By merging both these profiling techniques, you can create a more rounded and precise picture of your target market. This knowledge allows you to tailor your messaging and marketing strategies effectively, ensuring that you not only reach your audience but resonate deeply with them. As a result, you'll craft campaigns that don't just communicate but connect, driving long-term engagement and conversions.

**Niche Markets and Tailored Messaging** demands a deep dive into understanding uniquely defined segments of consumers and crafting messages that resonate specifically with them. It's not enough to create advertisements that appeal to everyone; you must recognize and address the nuanced needs and desires of small, targeted groups. This approach not only maximizes engagement but also builds a loyal customer base, one that feels your product or service was made specifically for them.

Targeting niche markets begins with extensive research. You need detailed demographic and psychographic profiles to understand who these consumers are, what they care about, and what influences their purchasing decisions. For instance, a sports equipment retailer targeting avid rock climbers will craft messages focusing on durability, safety, and performance rather than generalized sports features. The goal is to speak directly to the climbing community's concerns and interests in a language they understand.

Creating tailored messaging for niche markets involves breaking away from generic slogans and universal appeals. Instead, focus on personalizing the narrative to align with the specific experiences and passions of your target segment. If your market consists of eco-conscious consumers, your messaging should highlight sustainability, ethical sourcing, and environmental impact. These consumers will respond better to messages that reinforce their values and beliefs, making them more likely to choose your brand over competitors.

But how do you find these niche markets? Look for gaps in the broader market landscape where needs aren't being fully met. Often, these niches emerge from broader trend shifts or specific community developments. For instance, the rise of remote work has created a niche for ergonomic home office setups. Businesses that recognize this shift early can develop products and messages that address the specific needs of remote workers, such as comfort, productivity, and home office aesthetics.

Data analytics and social listening tools are invaluable in identifying emerging niches. By analyzing social media conversations, search trends, and consumer feedback, you can spot unaddressed needs and growing communities. Once you've identified these groups, segment your audience based on shared characteristics and behaviors. The more granular your segments, the more effectively you can tailor your messages. A one-size-fits-all approach rarely works in today's diverse and fragmented marketplace.

Next, consider leveraging influencer marketing to reach these niche communities. Influencers often have deep, authentic connections with their followers, making them ideal messengers for your tailored campaigns. For example, a fitness brand targeting yoga enthusiasts could partner with a well-known yoga instructor to showcase their products. The instructor's endorsement adds credibility and helps to foster trust with the niche audience.

Investing in personalized content creation is key. Whether through blogs, videos, or social media posts, the content should address specific pain points and interests of the niche market. Utilize storytelling to make the message more engaging. A success story of a small business owner using your software solution speaks directly to other small business owners who can see themselves in that narrative. Personalization extends beyond just content; even the channels you choose to communicate through should reflect the preferences of your niche audience.

Testing and optimizing your tailored messages cannot be overlooked. Initial campaigns may not hit the mark perfectly, but that's part of the process. Utilize A/B testing to experiment with different messages, visuals, and calls to action. Monitor how each variation performs and refine your strategy accordingly. Metrics like click-through rates (CTR), conversion rates, and engagement levels provide valuable insights into what resonates with your audience.

The language and tone of your messaging are equally crucial. Technical jargon might work well for a niche of professionals in a specific field but could alienate a broader audience. Conversely, colloquial language that feels authentic to a local or cultural community can strengthen bonds and enhance loyalty. Be mindful of these variations to avoid sounding either too aloof or overly casual.

Consider also the emotional triggers that drive your niche market's decisions. Emotional appeals can be incredibly powerful, whether it's the thrill of adventure for outdoor enthusiasts or the peace of mind for parents buying baby products. Understand the emotional landscape of your niche and weave that into your messaging. Sometimes, a heartfelt story or a sense of shared values can be more compelling than any statistical benefit.

Building a dedicated community around your niche market can amplify your efforts. Online forums, social media groups, and local events create platforms for consumers to engage with your brand and each other. These communities can become powerful advocates, sharing their satisfaction and fostering organic growth through word-of-mouth recommendations. As these groups grow, they offer even richer insights into your niche, helping you tailor your messaging even further.

Lastly, be ready to adapt. Niche markets can be incredibly dynamic, influenced by cultural shifts, technological advancements, and economic changes. Maintain a flexible strategy that allows you to pivot as necessary. Periodically revisit your market research, engage in social listening, and stay current with industry trends to ensure your tailored messaging continues to hit the mark.

In essence, mastering **Niche Markets and Tailored Messaging** requires a blend of detailed research, creative storytelling, and continuous optimization. It's about going beyond the surface to create meaningful connections that resonate deeply with specific groups. The rewards are significant – higher engagement rates, improved customer loyalty, and ultimately, a more robust bottom line.

# Chapter 7:
# Measuring Success: Metrics and Analytics

Navigating the intricate landscape of advertising demands a clear understanding of what defines success. Metrics and analytics serve as the compass, providing tangible insights into the performance of your campaigns. By defining key performance indicators (KPIs) that align with your business goals, you can quantify progress and identify areas for improvement. Utilize tools and techniques like A/B testing, data visualization, and real-time monitoring to fine-tune your strategies. An agile approach to adapting based on these insights ensures continuous growth and the ability to pivot when necessary. Remember, data isn't just numbers; it's a beacon guiding your decisions, empowering you to maximize impact and drive results.

## Defining KPIs for Advertising Campaigns

Key Performance Indicators (KPIs) are the pulse of your advertising campaigns, offering tangible metrics to gauge success. Defining the right KPIs is crucial for ensuring that your campaign meets its objectives and drives results. Begin by identifying your core goals—whether it's increasing brand awareness, driving website traffic, or boosting sales. Each goal should align with specific, measurable KPIs, such as click-through rates (CTR), conversion rates (CR), or return on ad spend (ROAS). Selecting appropriate KPIs enables you to focus on what's working, make data-driven decisions, and optimize your strategies in real-time. Essentially, well-defined KPIs act as a compass, guiding your campaign to achieve optimal performance and fostering continuous improvement.

**Tools and Techniques for Analysis** are essential for ensuring that advertising campaigns are not only launched effectively but also continually optimized for better performance. Understanding and leveraging the right tools and techniques can dramatically increase the impact of your marketing efforts, saving both time and money while maximizing results.

Marketing professionals today have a myriad of sophisticated tools at their disposal. Google Analytics, for example, is indispensable for understanding website traffic and user behavior. It provides detailed reports on metrics such as page views, bounce rates, and conversion paths. But Google Analytics is just the tip of the iceberg. Tools like SEMrush or Ahrefs allow you to delve into SEO and competitor analysis, giving insights into keyword opportunities and backlink strategies that can elevate your digital presence.

Another powerful tool in the arsenal is social media analytics. Platforms like Facebook Insights, Twitter Analytics, and LinkedIn Analytics offer in-depth data on user engagement, demographics, and the effectiveness of your content. These insights are critical for tailoring your social media strategies to better resonate with your target audience. Social listening tools such as Brandwatch or Hootsuite go one step further, tracking mentions, sentiment, and trends around your brand or industry, enabling you to engage proactively and meaningfully with your audience.

Don't underestimate the importance of Customer Relationship Management (CRM) systems, like Salesforce or HubSpot. These platforms aggregate customer data, track interactions, and manage relationships. The treasure trove of data housed in a CRM allows for segmented and highly personalized campaigns, ensuring that your messaging hits the right notes at the right times. CRM integration with automated marketing tools like Marketo or Mailchimp can streamline your efforts, reducing manual interventions and enhancing efficiency.

Data visualization tools such as Tableau or Power BI are game-changers when it comes to interpreting complex data. These tools allow you to create interactive, visual reports that make it easier to identify trends, anomalies, and opportunities. The ability to visually communicate data-driven insights is critical when presenting to stakeholders, ensuring that your findings are both impactful and understandable.

Traditional surveys and focus groups are still valuable, but today's digital landscape offers additional advanced methods for gathering consumer insights. Online survey tools like SurveyMonkey or Typeform make it easy to collect and analyze feedback from your audience. A/B testing platforms like Optimizely or Google Optimize allow for real-time experimentation with different campaign elements to determine what resonates most effectively with your audience. These tests can be applied to various components of your advertising, from email subject lines to landing page layouts, yielding valuable data on performance and preference.

The collection of data, however, is only part of the equation. Knowing how to analyze and interpret this data is what transforms it into actionable insights. Statistical analysis software like SPSS or SAS can handle complex data sets and provide rigorous statistical analysis. These programs help to identify patterns and correlations that may not be immediately apparent, offering deeper insights into consumer behavior and campaign performance.

Understanding the customer journey is another crucial aspect of effective analysis. Tools such as Hotjar or Crazy Egg offer heatmaps and session recordings that illuminate user behavior on your website. By knowing where users click, how far they scroll, and where they drop off, you can optimize your site for better user experience and higher conversion rates. These insights are invaluable for fine-tuning your landing pages, improving navigation, and ultimately increasing conversions.

In the realm of email marketing, tools like Mailchimp and Constant Contact provide not just the capability to send and automate emails, but also powerful analytics to track open rates, click-through rates, and conversion rates. Understanding these metrics can guide you in crafting more compelling subject lines, adjusting your send times, and segmenting your list for more personalized messaging. Analytics enable you to iterate and improve constantly, leading to more effective email campaigns over time.

Breakpoint analyses and cohort analyses are techniques that can further refine your understanding of campaign performance and customer behavior. Breakpoint analysis examines changes in your metrics over time to identify moments when significant shifts occur. This can help in attributing changes to specific campaigns or external factors. Cohort analysis, on the other hand, looks at groups of users who share a common characteristic, such as the date they signed up for a service, and tracks their behavior over time. This technique provides insights into user retention and customer lifetime value, critical metrics for long-term business success.

Moreover, aligning your metrics and key performance indicators (KPIs) with business objectives is paramount. It's important to ensure that the metrics you're tracking actually reflect the goals of your campaign and your broader marketing strategy. For instance, while vanity metrics like likes and shares might offer some insights into engagement, they don't necessarily correlate with sales or customer acquisition. Focus on actionable metrics that drive business growth, such as conversion rates, customer acquisition costs, and return on ad spend.

The integration of machine learning and artificial intelligence in analytics tools is paving the way for even more advanced insights and predictive analytics. Platforms like IBM Watson or Google Cloud AI offer capabilities that go beyond traditional analysis, enabling you to forecast trends, automate complex data processes, and discover deeper patterns. These advanced tools make it easier to anticipate customer needs, optimize marketing strategies, and achieve a higher degree of personalization.

Finally, keep in mind that the landscape of tools and techniques is ever-evolving. Staying abreast of the latest advancements and continuously adapting your approach is key to maintaining a competitive edge. Continuous learning and experimentation are integral to mastering the craft of data analysis in marketing.

In conclusion, the right tools and techniques for analysis can significantly boost the effectiveness of your advertising campaigns. Whether it's leveraging powerful analytics platforms, conducting precise A/B tests, utilizing sophisticated data visualization tools, or integrating AI for predictive insights, your approach to analysis can set you apart from the competition. By combining these methodologies with a deep understanding of your audience and clear alignment with business objectives, you'll be well-equipped to drive impactful and successful marketing initiatives.

**Adapting to Results** is a crucial practice for any marketing campaign. It's not just about launching a campaign and hoping it works; it's about continuously monitoring its performance and being ready to make changes based on the data you gather. This approach ensures that your efforts remain aligned with your objectives and, more importantly, that they resonate with your target audience.

Let's break this down. As marketing professionals, we need to understand that every campaign is an experiment. You align your strategies with certain hypotheses—perhaps you believe a specific emotional trigger will drive engagement, or that a unique headline will capture attention. But once the campaign is live, hard data will begin to tell you what truly works and what doesn't.

The first step in adapting to results is to establish clear metrics or KPIs (Key Performance Indicators). Typical KPIs might include click-through rates (CTR), conversion rates, engagement metrics such as likes, shares, and comments, or even more detailed metrics like customer acquisition cost (CAC) and lifetime value (LTV). These metrics should align with your overall campaign goals and give you a clear picture of performance.

Once your KPIs are set, the next step is to continually monitor these metrics. Many powerful tools are available today—Google Analytics, social media insights, CRM systems, and more. Regularly review the data these tools provide. If a particular metric isn't meeting your expectations, it's time to dig in and understand why. This ongoing analysis helps identify underperforming areas that need attention.

Now, onto the adaptation process. Suppose your data indicates that your advertisement isn't driving as many conversions as expected. This insight demands action. Instead of shutting down the campaign, look for ways to tweak it. Perhaps your call-to-action isn't compelling enough, or your target audience needs to be more accurately defined. Sometimes, a simple change—like modifying an image or headline—can significantly impact performance.

Furthermore, A/B testing is a powerful method for adapting to results. By running two versions of an ad simultaneously with slight variations, you can see what resonates more effectively with your audience. Whether it's testing different images, headlines, or even entire concepts, A/B testing allows you to make data-driven decisions. These insights not only benefit the current campaign but can inform future strategies as well.

Another essential aspect of adaptation is feedback loops. Engage with your audience directly through surveys, comments, and direct interactions. Sometimes, qualitative data can reveal insights that pure numbers can't. Understanding the sentiment behind the feedback will help you make informed decisions about what to adapt.

It's also vital to remain agile and flexible. Marketing professionals must get comfortable with the idea that no campaign is perfect from the start. The digital landscape, particularly, is fast-paced and ever-changing. A strategy that worked last month might not work today. Keeping a pulse on industry trends and being ready to pivot based on new data ensures that your campaigns remain relevant and effective.

Long-term success in advertising comes from this cycle of implementing, measuring, adapting, and optimizing. It's about learning from each campaign to improve continually. Even campaigns that perform well can always be fine-tuned for better results. For instance, a successful social media campaign might still reveal some age groups that didn't engage as expected. Investigate why and make adjustments in future campaigns to target these segments better.

Let's not forget collaboration. Share insights and data across your team, and encourage input from various stakeholders. This collective approach not only leads to better-optimized campaigns but also fosters a culture of constant improvement within your organization. Everyone becomes part of the process, from creative teams to data analysts.

In conclusion, **Adapting to Results** is an ongoing process that transforms data into actionable insights, driving continuous improvement. Embrace it as a fundamental aspect of your marketing strategy. Remember, the ability to pivot and enhance your efforts based on real-world performance is what ultimately sets successful businesses apart from the rest.

# Chapter 8:
# Ethical Advertising

Ethical advertising isn't just a nice-to-have; it's a cornerstone for building lasting relationships with your audience. By prioritizing honesty and integrity in your campaigns, you foster trust and loyalty, which can lead to sustained success. Running misleading ads might give you a quick boost, but it's a strategy that's bound to backfire. Instead, aim to educate and genuinely address your audience's needs. When consumers feel respected and well-informed, they're more likely to engage with and advocate for your brand. Remember, in an age where transparency is valued more than ever, ethical advertising isn't just the right thing to do—it's the smart thing to do.

## Responsibility to Consumers

As marketers, our fundamental duty is to ensure that our advertising practices serve the best interests of consumers while driving business objectives. Ethical advertising is about more than compliance with regulations; it's a commitment to fostering genuine, honest relationships with our audience. Consumers trust us to provide accurate information, protect their privacy, and respect their choices, and we must honor this trust. This means crafting messages that are truthful, non-deceptive, and considerate of the well-being of those we aim to reach. By prioritizing the consumer's interests, we not only build stronger, more loyal relationships but also set a standard for integrity that can elevate the entire industry. Aim to inspire, educate, and engage without misleading, for it is through responsible advertising that we can truly achieve meaningful success and long-term impact.

**Transparency and Trust Building** are the cornerstones of ethical advertising. In today's hyper-connected world, consumers have access to an abundance of information at their fingertips. They can research products, read reviews, and compare prices within minutes. With this level of access, it's more critical than ever for brands to prioritize honesty and openness in their communications. When a company is transparent about its practices, values, and products, it fosters a sense of trust and loyalty among its audience, making them more likely to choose and stick with that brand.

Consider the rise of social media, where consumers openly discuss their experiences with brands. A single negative review or perceived dishonesty can quickly go viral, damaging a brand's reputation. Conversely, brands that consistently demonstrate transparency are often met with positive engagement and word-of-mouth referrals. This not only helps in retaining existing customers but also attracts new ones.

One effective way to build trust through transparency is by being upfront about product details. This includes everything from the ingredients in a food item to the materials used in manufacturing a gadget. For instance, many companies now provide detailed sourcing information, allowing consumers to understand where their products come from and how they're made. This level of detail can reassure customers that they're making informed decisions, which is particularly important in today's environment where social and ecological consciousness is growing.

In addition to product transparency, honesty in advertising is essential. This means avoiding exaggerated claims or misleading information. When consumers feel misled, it not only affects their perception of the specific product but also taints their view of the brand as a whole. It's far more sustainable and beneficial in the long run to market products based on their genuine benefits and features. Authenticity resonates far more deeply with consumers than flashy but hollow claims.

To illustrate, take the example of a skincare company that promises "instant results." If the product doesn't deliver on this promise, customers are likely to feel deceived. On the other hand, if the company realistically describes the benefits, such as "visible improvements within four weeks with regular use," and the product meets these expectations, customers are more likely to be satisfied and remain loyal.

Customer interaction and communication also play a significant role in transparency and trust-building. Brands must be accessible and responsive. This means having active customer service channels where consumers can quickly and easily find answers to their queries or resolve issues. An excellent example is Zappos, which is known for its exceptional customer service. The company has built a reputation for being extremely responsive and transparent with customers, which in turn has cultivated a very loyal customer base.

Transparency goes beyond just customer service and product information; it extends to company values and business practices. Modern consumers are particularly attuned to issues such as corporate social responsibility, ethical labor practices, and environmental sustainability. Companies that are forthright about their efforts in these areas can gain a competitive edge. TOMS, for instance, has made its "One for One" mission—whereby the company donates a pair of shoes for every pair sold—a central part of its brand identity. This transparent CSR initiative has significantly boosted its market presence and consumer trust.

The impact of transparency on corporate culture shouldn't be overlooked either. Internally, fostering a culture of transparency can improve morale and productivity. When employees feel that they're part of an open and honest organization, they're more likely to be engaged and committed. This internal alignment between employee values and company ethos radiates outward, reinforcing the authenticity consumers seek.

Transparency must be an ongoing effort, not a one-off campaign. It needs to be integrated into every aspect of a business, from marketing to internal operations and customer interactions. Regular updates about product changes, company initiatives, and even setbacks can keep consumers in the loop and enhance their trust in the brand. Patagonia, for example, frequently updates its customers about its environmental initiatives and shares both successes and areas for improvement. This openness has helped solidify its reputation as a genuinely responsible brand.

Lastly, customers appreciate brands that admit their mistakes. When a company makes an error, acknowledging it honestly and promptly can actually strengthen consumer trust rather than diminish it. In 2016, Samsung recalled the Galaxy Note 7 due to battery issues that caused some units to catch fire. The company was swift to communicate the problem, take responsibility, and outline the steps they were taking to address it. While the recall was a significant setback, Samsung's transparent handling of the situation helped preserve its overall brand trust.

In summary, **Transparency and Trust Building** are pivotal in creating a strong bond with consumers. They require a commitment to honesty in product descriptions, advertising, customer interaction, and company practices. As we've seen, the benefits of maintaining transparency are manifold: higher customer retention, enhanced brand reputation, increased loyalty, and a competitive market edge. When consumers trust a brand, they're not just buying a product—they're buying into a relationship. Building that relationship through transparency is not just good ethics; it's good business.

# Chapter 9:
## The Future of Advertising

The future of advertising is an exhilarating landscape of emerging technologies and innovative strategies that promise to redefine how businesses connect with their audiences. Imagine a world where AI-driven personalization makes each consumer feel like the sole focus of a campaign, or where augmented reality turns ads into immersive experiences that engage like never before. As new platforms and trends continue to evolve, marketers will need to stay agile and adaptable, leveraging data-driven insights to craft compelling, relevant messages. This is not just about keeping up with change; it's about embracing it, pushing creative boundaries, and always staying one step ahead. To thrive, today's marketing professionals must be willing to experiment, learn, and pivot swiftly, ensuring they're not only part of the conversation but driving it forward.

### Emerging Technologies and Trends

As we look towards the future of advertising, it becomes evident that emerging technologies and current trends are reshaping the landscape in ways we could hardly imagine a decade ago. Artificial intelligence and machine learning are transforming how we analyze consumer data, predict behaviors, and personalize ad experiences. Virtual reality and augmented reality offer immersive experiences that make consumers feel like part of the brand's story, while blockchain technology ensures transparency and trust in digital advertising. Additionally, the proliferation of smart devices is leading to new, interactive forms of content delivery, thus requiring brands to be ever more agile and innovative. To stay ahead, advertising professionals must embrace these technological advancements, anticipating and adapting to shifts in consumer expectations and behaviors. This dynamic approach isn't just about staying relevant; it's about leading the charge in an industry that's constantly evolving.

**Adaptation and Innovation in Marketing Strategies** is more essential now than ever before due to the rapid pace of technological advancement and shifting consumer behaviors. Businesses that fail to innovate risk becoming obsolete in a market landscape that prioritizes agility and forward-thinking. To stay competitive, it's crucial to integrate both adaptation and innovation into your marketing strategies seamlessly.

Start by understanding that adaptation involves more than just small tweaks to your existing methods; it requires a fundamental shift in mindset. You need to be receptive to change and quick to implement new ideas. Traditional marketing paradigms no longer suffice in a world driven by instantaneous digital interactions. Embrace data, consumer feedback, and technological tools to inform your strategies. For instance, leveraging artificial intelligence and machine learning can help predict consumer behavior more accurately, allowing for more personalized and effective campaigns.

Innovation, on the other hand, involves creating something entirely new and different. This could mean the development of a revolutionary product, the adoption of state-of-the-art technology, or the application of completely unique marketing tactics. Think about how disruptive technologies like blockchain, augmented reality (AR), and virtual reality (VR) are changing the advertising space. These technologies not only offer novel ways to engage with customers but also create immersive experiences that can significantly enhance brand appeal.

Let's consider the potential of AR in retail marketing. AR allows customers to visualize products in their real-world environments before making a purchase. This technology can transform a standard online shopping experience into an interactive adventure, fostering a deeper emotional connection with your brand. Similarly, VR can be used for training purposes, giving prospective customers a firsthand experience of a product or service.

However, innovation isn't only about tech. The rise of purpose-driven brands underscores how values and social responsibility can be integrated into marketing strategies. Being transparent about your company's ethical practices and commitment to societal issues can resonate deeply with today's conscious consumers. This is especially pertinent in creating brand loyalty among Millennials and Gen Z, who prioritize authenticity and ethical considerations in their purchasing decisions.

The flexibility to adapt and innovate also entails the ability to pivot quickly in response to market trends and economic shifts. One vivid example is the surge in remote working due to unforeseen events like the COVID-19 pandemic. Companies that successfully pivoted their marketing strategies to address the needs of home-bound consumers not only survived but thrived. Virtual events, webinars, and online consultations became indispensable tools, and those who leveraged these mediums were able to maintain, if not expand, their customer bases.

To integrate innovation effectively, consider adopting a test-and-learn approach. This involves experimenting with different marketing tactics, measuring their success, and iterating based on the results. A/B testing in digital campaigns, for instance, can provide actionable insights into what resonates most with your target audience. By being open to experimentation, you create a culture that values continuous improvement and learning, empowering your team to seize new opportunities as they arise.

Another area ripe for innovation is personalization. Today's consumers expect brands to understand their unique preferences and provide tailored experiences. Utilizing customer data to segment your audience allows for highly targeted campaigns that speak directly to individual needs and desires. Personalization engines, which utilize machine learning algorithms, can automate this process, delivering customized recommendations in real-time.

On the creative front, harness the power of storytelling to differentiate your brand. Stories have the power to evince emotions and create meaningful connections, making your messaging more memorable. Craft narratives that reflect your brand's values, mission, and vision. Turn customer testimonials and success stories into engaging content, blending them with visually compelling graphics and videos to capture attention across various platforms.

Indeed, the convergence of traditional and digital media offers fertile ground for both adaptation and innovation. Integrating these platforms can amplify your reach and impact. For example, using digital analytics to inform your print campaigns can enhance their precision and effectiveness. Meanwhile, content initially designed for traditional media can be repurposed for digital channels, providing a consistent brand message while maximizing resource efficiency.

Finally, building a robust cross-functional team that encourages collaboration and diversity of thought is paramount. Bringing together individuals with various skill sets and perspectives fosters a rich environment for creative problem-solving. Encourage your team to think beyond conventional boundaries and to be bold in proposing new ideas. Celebrate successes, learn from failures, and maintain an unwavering focus on continual growth and improvement.

In summary, **Adaptation and Innovation in Marketing Strategies** are interconnected pathways to sustained success in an ever-evolving marketplace. By staying flexible, embracing new technologies, prioritizing personalized experiences, and fostering a culture of continuous learning, your business can successfully navigate the complexities of the modern market landscape. Don't just keep up with the changes; be the force that drives them.

# Chapter 10:
## Budgeting for Maximum Impact

Budgeting for maximum impact isn't just about spending wisely; it's about strategically allocating your resources to ensure that every dollar spent drives meaningful results. Businesses must evaluate the potential return on investment for each platform and method, balancing cost with the potential reach and engagement. It's essential to prioritize high-impact, cost-effective channels that align with your target audience's habits and preferences. By continuously analyzing performance data and adapting your budget allocation accordingly, you ensure that your campaigns remain effective and financially sustainable. This proactive approach to budget management allows you to stay agile in a constantly evolving market landscape, maximizing both your advertising spend and overall campaign success.

### Allocating Resources Wisely

When it comes to maximizing your advertising budget, smart allocation of resources is key. This isn't just about spending less—it's about spending strategically. Prioritize your investments by focusing on high-impact areas that deliver measurable results. For instance, blend digital platforms that offer precise targeting with traditional media that has a broad reach. Always keep an eye on your metrics and be ready to pivot your strategy if something's not working. From leveraging cost-effective social media campaigns to exploring niche markets, the goal is to make every dollar count. Efficient resource allocation empowers you to amplify your brand's message without unnecessary expenditure, ensuring you get the best bang for your buck.

**Cost-Effective Platforms and Methods** can truly transform your advertising practice, regardless of your budget constraints. It's not just about stretching your dollar further, but about strategically choosing tools and methods that maximize your returns. In today's rapidly evolving advertising landscape, getting the best bang for your buck is both art and science.

First, let's talk about social media platforms. Without a doubt, platforms like Facebook, Instagram, LinkedIn, and Twitter are goldmines for cost-effective advertising. Why? They allow for precise targeting, ensuring your ad dollars are spent reaching the exact demographic you desire. Facebook Ads, for example, allows you to define your audience based on criteria such as location, age, interests, and behavior. The same goes for LinkedIn, which is particularly useful for B2B marketing.

But it's not just about choosing the right platform; it's about leveraging its features. Take advantage of the tools these platforms provide. Instagram Stories and Reels, for instance, are cost-effective methods to engage audiences, often seeing higher engagement rates compared to traditional posts. Create interactive content, use polls, and incorporate user-generated content to foster a sense of community and engagement.

Another indispensable method is content marketing. Unlike traditional advertising, content marketing focuses on creating valuable content that attracts and retains a clearly defined audience. Blogs, whitepapers, ebooks, and webinars are excellent avenues. The key lies in understanding your audience's pain points and addressing them through high-quality content. This approach not only reduces costs over time but also builds credibility and trust with your audience, which is priceless.

Search engine optimization (SEO) should not be overlooked when discussing cost-effectiveness. Optimizing your website to rank high in search engine results can lead to significant organic traffic, reducing the need for paid ads. Simple SEO practices such as keyword research, meta tags optimization, and producing high-quality backlinks can go a long way. Tools like Google Analytics and SEMrush offer valuable insights into your website's performance, guiding your SEO efforts effectively.

Email marketing remains one of the most cost-effective platforms. With a high return on investment (ROI) — $38 for every $1 spent, according to some studies — it's hard to ignore. Build a segmented email list, personalize your messages, and employ automation tools to stay connected with your audience. Employ A/B testing to refine your messages, subject lines, and formats continuously. Platforms like Mailchimp and Constant Contact provide robust tools to streamline your email campaigns at reasonable costs.

Don't underestimate the power of partnerships and collaborations. Working with influencers or other businesses in your industry can help you reach new audiences more efficiently. Micro-influencers, who have smaller but more engaged followings, are often more cost-effective than big-name celebrities. By offering product exchanges or profit-sharing models, you can run partnership campaigns without heavy financial outlay.

Video content is another highly engaging and cost-effective method. With the rise of platforms like TikTok and the increasing preference for video content on social media, creating short, engaging videos can provide substantial reach at a lower cost. Tools like Animoto and InVideo allow even those with limited budgets to produce professional-quality video content.

Leveraging user-generated content can also be highly effective. Encourage your existing customers to share their experiences with your products or services through photo or video contests. This not only builds community but also provides authentic, cost-efficient content for your campaigns. Highlighting real customer testimonials adds an element of trust that paid advertising often can't achieve.

The rapid evolution of technology has introduced programmatic advertising, which uses automated processes to buy and place ads. This method can significantly reduce costs and improve targeting by using data analytics to place ads where they are most likely to be effective. Programmatic advertising platforms like Google Display Network help you cut costs while maximizing reach.

Consider exploring native advertising as well, which involves placing ads in a format that fits seamlessly into the user experience. Sponsored content on news websites or social media feeds tends to perform better and at a lower cost than traditional banner ads, as these ads don't disrupt the user experience and are more engaging.

Another avenue worth exploring is community-based platforms like Reddit and Quora. While these might not be the first platforms that come to mind when planning advertising campaigns, their highly engaged communities can offer niche targeting opportunities. Advertise within relevant subreddits or answer questions on Quora related to your industry to position yourself as a thought leader.

Finally, let's not forget the importance of continuous learning and adaptation. The digital advertising landscape is always shifting, and staying informed about the latest trends and tools can offer an edge over competitors. Investing in courses, attending webinars, and keeping up with industry news through blogs and forums can be invaluable. Allocate a portion of your budget to testing new methods and platforms; what works today may not be as effective tomorrow, and vice versa.

In conclusion, the key to utilizing cost-effective platforms and methods lies in understanding your audience, leveraging existing tools and features, and remaining agile. Combining various strategies such as social media, content marketing, SEO, email marketing, partnerships, video content, user-generated content, programmatic advertising, native advertising, and community engagement can help you optimize your budget while achieving maximum impact. Remember, it's not just about spending less, but about spending smart.

# Chapter 11:
# Creativity in Advertising

Creativity in advertising is the spark that turns good campaigns into unforgettable ones. It's about breaking the mold and daring to be different, pushing the boundaries of what's considered "safe." Whether it's through memorable storytelling, captivating visuals, or innovative use of media, creativity can captivate audiences and leave a lasting impression. It involves thinking outside the box and finding novel solutions to engage consumers in a crowded marketplace. To innovate effectively, one must combine a deep understanding of the brand and its audience with a willingness to experiment and take calculated risks. The greatest campaigns are often born from moments of bold creativity, proving that a unique idea can be more powerful than the most substantial budget. Inspirational case studies from the advertising world emphasize that when creativity meets strategy, the results can be extraordinary, driving not just awareness but also emotional connection and loyalty. Remember, in advertising, as in life, fortune often favors the bold.

## Breaking the Mold with Innovative Ideas

In today's fast-paced advertising world, breaking the mold with innovative ideas is not just an option but a necessity. By stepping outside the conventional boundaries, marketers can capture attention, spark curiosity, and drive engagement like never before. Innovative advertising is about more than just being different; it's about understanding your audience at a deeper level and resonating with their needs and desires in unexpected ways. To inspire groundbreaking campaigns, one must cultivate an environment that encourages risk-taking and creativity, challenging the status quo while remaining true to the brand's core values. After all, those who dare to think differently often find themselves leading the pack, setting new benchmarks for success in the industry.

**Case Studies of Successful Campaigns** offer a treasure trove of insights for anyone in the marketing and advertising space looking to replicate success. When executed well, these campaigns demonstrate a deep understanding of the target audience, a mastery of various media channels, and a creative approach that captures attention and drives action. Let's delve into several iconic advertising campaigns that have not only boosted sales for their respective companies but also left indelible marks on the advertising landscape.

The first campaign worth highlighting is the famed "Share a Coke" initiative by Coca-Cola. Launched in Australia in 2011, the campaign aimed to breathe new life into the brand by connecting with consumers on a personal level. Coca-Cola replaced its iconic logo with popular first names on bottles and cans, encouraging people to "share" a Coke with friends or family. This simple yet powerful idea capitalized on the human need for personalization and social connection. The result? A significant increase in sales and brand engagement. Coca-Cola saw a 7% increase in consumption among young adults in Australia, and the campaign was subsequently rolled out in over 80 countries.

One of the critical success factors was the multi-channel approach that included traditional media, social media, and experiential marketing. People flocked to social platforms to share images of their personalized Coke bottles, effectively becoming brand ambassadors. Coca-Cola also set up kiosks where customers could create custom labels, further deepening their engagement. The key takeaway from this campaign is the importance of personalization and leveraging social proof to amplify reach.

Another shining example is the Old Spice "The Man Your Man Could Smell Like" campaign. In a bid to reposition Old Spice as a modern, desirable brand for younger audiences, Wieden+Kennedy created a series of humorous ads featuring the charismatic Isaiah Mustafa. The ads broke from traditional male grooming clichés by using humor and an unconventional narrative style. The blend of sharp wit, memorable catchphrases, and internet-friendly content catapulted Old Spice to viral fame.

The campaign's impact was measurable and profound. Sales of Old Spice body wash rose by 125% within the first six months. The content strategy, relying heavily on digital channels—especially YouTube—allowed the campaign to reach an extensive audience at a relatively low cost. Moreover, the brand leveraged social media interactions, responding to fans in real-time with personalized video replies. This not only extended the campaign's lifespan but also increased consumer engagement manifold. Humor and a fresh narrative approach, coupled with real-time engagement, played a crucial role in the campaign's success.

Moving to the realm of digital marketing, Airbnb's "Made Possible by Hosts" campaign showcases the power of authenticity and community storytelling. Launched in 2020, the campaign highlighted true stories from Airbnb hosts and guests, emphasizing the unique, personal experiences made possible through the platform. By focusing on real-life moments and the community aspect, Airbnb managed to build trust and emotional connections with its audience during a time when travel was fraught with uncertainty due to the COVID-19 pandemic.

The campaign utilized a multi-channel strategy, featuring video content across social media, television, and even long-form formats like podcasts. However, what made it particularly impactful was the user-generated content. Encouraging hosts and guests to share their stories helped to create a sense of belonging and authenticity, enhancing the campaign's relatability and reach. The lesson here is the value of leveraging authentic stories and community to build brand trust and emotional connections.

Another noteworthy example is Nike's "Just Do It" campaign, which has become synonymous with the brand itself. Originally launched in 1988, the campaign aimed to inspire everyday athletes to push their limits, regardless of their starting point. The slogan "Just Do It" is not only motivational but also highly inclusive, resonating with a broad audience. This campaign has maintained its relevance for decades through continuous adaptation and powerful endorsements from sports icons like Michael Jordan, Serena Williams, and Colin Kaepernick.

The long-term success of the "Just Do It" campaign can be attributed to its simple, yet versatile message. It has the ability to adapt to various cultural moments and societal changes, thereby staying relevant. Nike has consistently used this campaign to support causes that align with its brand values, such as racial equality and women's empowerment, which further solidifies its position as a brand with a conscience. The primary takeaway from Nike's example is the importance of a strong, adaptable slogan that can serve as a North Star for various marketing initiatives over time.

Next, we should look at Dove's "Real Beauty" campaign, which aimed to broaden the conversation around beauty standards. Launched in 2004, the campaign featured women of various sizes, ages, and ethnicities, challenging the unrealistic portrayals of beauty often seen in media. Dove took a risk by diverging from conventional beauty advertising, but it paid off in spades.

The campaign struck a chord globally, leading to a sales increase from $2.5 billion to $4 billion in the first ten years. Dove's commitment to this cause went beyond ads, extending to educational initiatives and partnerships with organizations like the World Association of Girl Guides and Girl Scouts. By promoting self-esteem and body positivity, Dove successfully positioned itself as a brand that cares about its consumers' well-being, building long-term loyalty. This case study underscores the power of taking a stand on important social issues and aligning them with brand values to build a deeper connection with the audience.

The ALS Association's "Ice Bucket Challenge" is another example of a campaign that not only achieved its immediate goals but also sparked a global movement. Initiated in 2014 to raise awareness and funds for amyotrophic lateral sclerosis (ALS), the campaign encouraged participants to dump a bucket of ice water over their heads, post a video of it online, and challenge others to do the same or donate to the cause. The campaign went viral, with celebrities, athletes, and everyday people participating.

In just eight weeks, the Ice Bucket Challenge raised over $115 million for ALS research. The campaign's success lay in its simplicity, participatory nature, and the leverage of social networks. By making it easy to participate and nominating others to join, the campaign created a sense of community and collective action. The key lesson here is the effectiveness of user-generated content and leveraging social networks to amplify a cause.

These case studies highlight some core principles of successful advertising campaigns. First, understanding and connecting with your target audience on a personal and emotional level is crucial. Whether it's through personalization, humor, authenticity, or social impact, the best campaigns resonate deeply with their audience. Second, a multichannel approach that integrates traditional and digital media can significantly extend the reach and impact of a campaign. Lastly, adaptability and alignment with brand values ensure long-term relevance and foster deeper connections with consumers.

By understanding the nuances of these successful campaigns, marketing professionals can glean valuable strategies and adapt them to their own initiatives. The fusion of creativity, strategy, and execution showcased in these campaigns exemplifies the transformative power of well-crafted advertising. These principles, when applied thoughtfully, can lead to remarkable results, transforming not just sales, but also how a brand is perceived

# Chapter 12:
## Building a Brand Through Advertising

Building a brand through advertising goes beyond simply promoting products; it's about creating an identity that resonates and lingers in the minds of consumers. Effective advertising shapes how people perceive your brand, making it essential to establish a robust and consistent brand identity. This involves a meticulous blend of visual elements, messaging, and strategic placement that collectively tell a coherent story about who you are and what you stand for. Focus on long-term strategies rather than quick wins to foster brand loyalty that holds up over time. By investing in storytelling and emotional connections, you create memorable experiences that continuously attract and engage your audience, ultimately transforming everyday consumers into passionate advocates for your brand.

### Establishing a Strong Brand Identity

Establishing a strong brand identity is the linchpin of any successful advertising strategy, playing a pivotal role in setting you apart in a crowded marketplace. By honing your brand's unique voice, visual elements, and core values, you create a cohesive and memorable experience for your audience. This identity becomes the foundation upon which all advertising efforts are built, harmonizing messages across various platforms and fostering a deep emotional connection with consumers. It's crucial to maintain consistency while also allowing for a degree of flexibility to adapt to changing market dynamics. Mastery in this area ensures that your brand not only gains initial recognition but also garners long-term loyalty and trust. Remember, a robust brand identity isn't just about logos and slogans; it's about encapsulating the essence of what you stand for and effectively communicating that to the world.

**Long-Term Strategies for Brand Loyalty** are the secret weapon in a competitive marketplace. To inspire undying loyalty, you can't rely solely on one-off promotions or flashy ad campaigns. You must cultivate a deeper connection with your audience, turning casual customers into fervent brand advocates. But how do you achieve this transformation? Let's explore a multifaceted approach that combines emotional engagement, consistent value delivery, and active community building.

First and foremost, emotional engagement is crucial. People remember how you make them feel more than they remember the specifics of what you do. Strong emotional ties fortify a consumer's connection to your brand. To accomplish this, think about the emotional triggers that resonate with your target audience. Tailor your messaging to align with their core values and aspirations. For instance, brands like Apple have mastered this art by creating a narrative around innovation, creativity, and a sense of belonging.

Think about your brand's story. How can you weave personal anecdotes, customer testimonials, and mission-driven content into your communication strategy? Storytelling isn't just about the 'what'; it's about the 'why.' Share your brand's journey, highlighting the challenges and triumphs that have shaped your mission. This transparency not only humanizes your brand but also makes it easier for customers to identify with you on a personal level.

Providing consistent value is another cornerstone. Consumers are more likely to stick around when they see your brand as a continual source of benefit. Evaluate your offerings and make sure they evolve with customer needs. Loyalty programs and exclusive memberships can provide added value that makes customers feel special and prioritized. For instance, Starbucks' rewards program keeps customers coming back by offering personalized offers and incentives that cater to their purchasing habits.

But value isn't just about discounts and perks. It's about genuine commitment to customer satisfaction. Make it easy for your consumers to communicate their needs, complaints, and feedback. Use this input to refine your products and services continuously. Respond promptly and effectively when issues arise, demonstrating that you value their patronage as much as their dollars. Personalized customer service can create memorable experiences that customers will want to repeat.

Another strategy involves developing a sense of community around your brand. This transcends transactions and fosters a shared identity among your customers. Leverage both online and offline platforms to build this community. Social media groups, forums, and live events can be powerful tools for fostering a sense of belonging. Encourage user-generated content and create spaces where customers can share their experiences and stories related to your brand.

Nurture these communities by engaging directly with members. Participate in conversations, acknowledge contributions, and occasionally offer exclusive insights or previews of upcoming products. When customers feel they are part of an insider group, their loyalty deepens, and they become more likely to advocate on your behalf.

Additionally, consider the role of educational content in establishing long-term loyalty. When you educate your audience, you empower them. This can range from how-to guides and webinars to in-depth articles and videos that align with your product or service. Educational content showcases your expertise, making you a go-to resource in your industry. It's a win-win: customers get valuable information, and you establish your brand as an authority.

Furthermore, don't underestimate the power of corporate social responsibility. Today's consumers are socially conscious and prefer to support businesses that give back to the community and practice ethical standards. This means your brand's values should align with those of your audience. Whether it's through sustainable practices, charitable donations, or community initiatives, demonstrating a commitment to making the world a better place can significantly enhance brand loyalty.

Aligning your brand with social causes also offers opportunities for collaboration and storytelling. Partner with organizations that share your values and create campaigns that highlight your collective impact. This not only boosts your brand's credibility but also builds a deeper, purpose-driven connection with your audience.

Utilizing data analytics effectively can further refine and enhance your long-term brand loyalty strategies. Detailed insights into consumer behavior help you anticipate needs, preferences, and pain points. Tailor your marketing efforts based on these insights to provide increasingly personalized and relevant experiences. Remember, the more you understand your customers, the better you can serve them.

Regularly review and analyze customer data to identify trends and shifts in behavior. This enables you to stay ahead of the curve, adapting your strategies to meet evolving demands. Use surveys, feedback forms, and in-depth interviews to gain a deeper understanding of your audience's mindsets and motivations.

Lastly, never underestimate the importance of innovation. The brand landscape is constantly evolving, and staying stagnant can erode the loyalty you've worked so hard to build. Always be on the lookout for new trends, technologies, and strategies that can enhance your brand's appeal. Whether it's through new product offerings, adopting cutting-edge technology, or refining customer service practices, continual innovation keeps your brand relevant and exciting.

For example, the rise of artificial intelligence (AI) and machine learning offers novel ways to personalize customer interactions further. Implementing chatbots for instant customer support or using predictive analytics to tailor product recommendations are just a few ways to leverage these technologies. By staying ahead of the technological curve, you ensure that your brand remains fresh, modern, and customer-centric.

To sum up, **Long-Term Strategies for Brand Loyalty** are built on a foundation of emotional engagement, consistent value delivery, community building, educational content, corporate social responsibility, data-driven personalization, and continuous innovation. By integrating these elements, your brand can create an enduring bond with consumers that lasts well beyond any single transaction. Remember, brand loyalty isn't bought; it's earned through consistent, authentic, and meaningful interactions.

# The Path Forward in Advertising Excellence

As we've journeyed through the intricacies of advertising, it's clear that achieving excellence in this field is no small feat. From understanding human psychology to leveraging emerging technologies, the landscape of advertising is as dynamic as the shifting sands. But while the tools and platforms may evolve, the core principles remain. At the heart of exceptional advertising lies the unwavering commitment to connect meaningfully with your audience.

Advertising is not merely about selling products; it's about telling a story that resonates with people's emotions and aspirations. It's about crafting messages that cut through the noise and speak directly to the core of your audience's desires. This requires a nuanced understanding of both the art and science of communication. Emotional triggers and cognitive biases play a crucial role in shaping consumer behavior, and it's imperative to harness these psychological insights to create compelling campaigns.

With the rise of digital platforms, the opportunities for innovation have exploded. Social media, SEO, content marketing, and influencers are not just buzzwords—these are potent tools that, when utilized effectively, can amplify your brand's reach and impact. However, it's vital to integrate these with traditional media to create cohesive and multifaceted campaigns that leave a lasting impression.

Another cornerstone of advertising excellence is understanding and segmenting your audience. By delving deep into demographic and psychographic profiling, you can tailor your messaging to resonate with specific niches. This precision in targeting not only enhances engagement but also builds stronger, more personalized connections with your audience. It's about delivering the right message to the right people at the right time.

In our pursuit of excellence, we must also measure success meticulously. Defining clear KPIs, utilizing advanced analytics tools, and adapting to the results are critical steps in refining your strategies. Data-driven decision-making allows for continuous improvement and optimization of your campaigns, ensuring that you're always moving in the right direction.

Ethics in advertising cannot be overstressed. As custodians of public influence, we bear a significant responsibility to uphold transparency and trust. Ethical advertising builds long-term relationships with consumers and fosters brand loyalty. It's not just about following regulations but about genuinely caring for the well-being of your audience.

The future of advertising is promising, with emerging technologies like AI, augmented reality, and programmatic advertising presenting exciting new avenues. Adaptation and innovation are key to staying relevant in this ever-evolving landscape. Embrace these technologies with an open mind and a forward-thinking attitude, always remaining adaptable to change.

Resource allocation is another critical aspect. You must budget wisely to maximize impact. Opt for cost-effective platforms and methods that align with your campaign goals. Being strategic about where and how you spend your budget can significantly influence the outcomes of your advertising efforts.

Creativity remains at the core of breakthrough advertising. Innovative ideas that challenge the status quo position your brand as a leader in the industry. Studying successful case studies can provide valuable insights and inspire your creative process. Always aim to break the mold and set new benchmarks for creativity and engagement.

Building a robust brand through advertising entails establishing a strong identity and crafting long-term strategies that foster brand loyalty. Consistency, authenticity, and a deep understanding of your brand's values will guide your efforts in creating lasting impressions.

The path forward in advertising excellence is paved with challenges and opportunities. It demands a relentless focus on understanding human behavior, leveraging technology, ethical practices, creativity, strategic planning, and continuous learning. By embracing these principles, you're not just creating advertisements; you're crafting experiences that resonate, inspire, and drive action.

As you move forward, remember that the journey of advertising excellence is ongoing. Stay curious, stay innovative, and most importantly, stay committed to connecting with your audience in ways that are meaningful and impactful. The future is yours to shape, and with the right mindset and strategies, the possibilities are limitless.

# Appendix A:
## Appendix

The Appendix section provides additional information and resources to enhance the main content of the book. This section serves as a valuable reference for marketing professionals, business owners, salespeople, product managers, students, educators, communication specialists, advertisers, market researchers, entrepreneurial enthusiasts, and anyone with a keen interest in the psychology of persuasion. It aims to support the educational goals, skill enhancement, and creative inspiration discussed throughout the chapters.

## A: Advertising Regulation and Compliance

Understanding regulation and compliance is crucial in advertising. Advertising professionals must be diligent about adhering to legal standards and ethical practices to maintain credibility and build consumer trust. The information in this section clarifies the rules and guidelines set by governing bodies, such as the Federal Trade Commission (FTC) in the United States, and outlines best practices for ensuring all advertising efforts are compliant.

- **Regulatory Bodies:** Overview of key regulatory bodies responsible for overseeing advertising practices in various regions.

- **Legal Requirements:** Explanation of the fundamental legal requirements every advertiser should be aware of to avoid penalties.

- **Ethical Guidelines:** Insight into ethical considerations and best practices for transparent and truthful advertising.

- **Case Studies:** Real-world examples highlighting the consequences of non-compliance and the benefits of adhering to standards.

Adhering to these guidelines not only safeguards businesses from legal repercussions but also bolsters consumer confidence and fosters long-term relationships. Marketing professionals are encouraged to stay informed and proactive about changes in regulation to ensure their strategies remain effective and compliant.

This appendix is just a starting point; professionals should refer to official resources and legal advisors for comprehensive and up-to-date information. Continuous learning and adaptation are key in the dynamic landscape of advertising regulations.

Utilize this appendix as a guide to navigate the complex world of advertising law and ethics, and always strive for responsible and impactful advertising practices.

## A: Advertising Regulation and Compliance

Advertising regulation and compliance might seem like a dry subject, but it's the bedrock that ensures the integrity and effectiveness of the entire industry. Without proper regulation, the advertising landscape would be chaotic, potentially deceptive, and harmful to consumers. Let's dive into why understanding and adhering to these regulations isn't just a legal requirement but a critical component in building a reputable brand and fostering consumer trust.

First and foremost, advertising laws and regulations are designed to protect consumers. Governments and regulatory bodies worldwide have established guidelines to ensure that advertisements do not mislead or exploit the public. These regulations cover a wide range of issues, from false claims and deceptive practices to ensuring that endorsements are genuine. Adhering to these rules helps marketers avoid hefty fines and legal action, but it also plays a significant role in maintaining consumer trust, which is invaluable in the long-term success of any brand.

One key aspect of advertising regulation is truth in advertising. Truth in advertising mandates that the claims made in advertisements must not be misleading or deceptive. This includes ensuring that facts presented in ads are substantiated and not exaggerated. For instance, a skincare product that claims to erase wrinkles must have credible scientific evidence to back up such a claim. Misleading consumers can not only result in significant fines but can also damage a brand's reputation beyond repair.

Moreover, disclosure is another crucial element in advertising compliance. Whether it's a paid endorsement or sponsored content, it's essential to disclose such relationships transparently. The Federal Trade Commission (FTC) in the United States, for instance, has guidelines that require influencers to clearly indicate their commercial relationships. This transparency helps maintain a level playing field and allows consumers to make informed decisions.

Different countries have different advertising regulations, and it's vital for marketers working in international markets to be aware of this. In some countries, the rules surrounding advertising to children are particularly stringent. Ads targeting children must be carefully crafted to avoid exploitation, and in many jurisdictions, certain products cannot be advertised to young audiences at all. Adhering to these regulations not only ensures legal compliance but also represents a commitment to ethical advertising practices.

In addition, digital advertising has brought new challenges and opportunities for regulation. Online ads are subject to the same truth-in-advertising standards as traditional media, but the rapid technological changes can make compliance more complex. Marketers must stay up-dated with the latest regulations governing digital spaces, such as the General Data Protection Regulation (GDPR) in the European Union, which enforces strict rules on how personal data is used in advertising.

For example, behavioral advertising, which targets users based on their browsing habits, must comply with privacy regulations. This involves obtaining explicit consent from users before collecting and utilizing their data. Failure to comply can lead to significant legal consequences and loss of consumer trust. Therefore, it's crucial for advertisers to integrate compliance checks into their campaign strategies from the outset.

The self-regulation by industry bodies also plays a crucial role. Organizations like the Advertising Self-Regulatory Council (ASRC) in the United States or the Advertising Standards Authority (ASA) in the United Kingdom set industry standards and offer a framework for ethical advertising. These bodies often act faster than governmental regulators and can address new advertising methods more promptly. Thus, staying engaged with industry self-regulatory organizations can provide additional guidance and ensure one remains on the right side of advertising laws.

Compliance is not just about avoiding penalties—it's also about building a reputable brand. Companies that consistently adhere to advertising regulations are more likely to earn the trust and loyalty of their consumers. Ethical advertising practices demonstrate a commitment to honesty and integrity, which can significantly enhance a brand's image and standing in the market.

Moreover, in industries like pharmaceuticals, financial services, and food and beverages, regulatory compliance is even more stringent due to the potential impacts on consumers' health and financial well-being. Advertisers in these sectors must navigate a maze of specific rules and ensure their campaigns undergo rigorous scrutiny before going live. Non-compliance in these areas can result in not only financial penalties but also severe harm to consumers, leading to long-lasting ramifications for the brand.

For instance, pharmaceutical ads require an abundance of disclaimers and must adhere to precise regulations regarding the information presented about the product's risks and benefits. Financial service advertisements must avoid making misleading claims that could potentially defraud or mislead investors. The stakes in these industries are particularly high, making regulatory compliance an essential aspect of the advertising process.

In conclusion, advertising regulation and compliance are indispensable aspects of creating responsible, ethical, and successful advertising campaigns. Beyond the legal ramifications, compliance fosters consumer trust and builds a reputable brand. It necessitates a proactive approach, constant vigilance, and a deep understanding of the ever-evolving regulatory landscape. By embedding these principles into your advertising strategies, you can ensure that your campaigns not only comply with the law but also resonate with integrity and transparency, setting the stage for long-term success.

## B: Glossary of Advertising Terms

In the world of advertising, knowledge is power. Understanding the terminology is crucial for navigating the industry and crafting compelling campaigns. Below, you'll find a comprehensive glossary of advertising terms to enhance your understanding and proficiency in this dynamic field.

- **A/B Testing:** A method of comparing two versions of a marketing asset to identify which one performs better. Often used in digital advertising to optimize campaigns.

- **Ad Copy:** The text component of an advertisement. Good ad copy clearly communicates the message and persuades the audience to take action.

- **Ad Placement:** The process of determining where an ad will appear, whether it be on social media platforms, websites, print media, or other channels.

- **Audience Segmentation:** Dividing a broad consumer or business market into sub-groups of consumers based on shared characteristics such as demographics, psychographics, and behaviors.

- **Brand Awareness:** The extent to which consumers are familiar with the qualities or image of a particular brand. High brand awareness often leads to higher sales.

- **Call to Action (CTA):** A prompt in an advertisement that tells the audience to take a specific action, such as "Buy Now," "Sign Up," or "Learn More."

- **Click-Through Rate (CTR):** The ratio of users who click on an advertisement to the number of total users who view it. It is a key metric in assessing the effectiveness of online ads.

- **Consumer Behavior:** The study of how individuals make decisions to spend their available resources on consumption-related items. Understanding this helps in crafting persuasive ads.

- **Cost Per Click (CPC):** A digital advertising model where advertisers pay a fee each time one of their ads is clicked. It is used to drive traffic to websites.

- **Creative Brief:** A document that outlines the strategy, goals, and key points for an advertising campaign. It serves as a guide for designers and copywriters.

- **Demographic Targeting:** Tailoring advertising efforts based on demographic factors like age, gender, income, and education level to better reach a specific audience.

- **Display Advertising:** A type of online advertising that comes in several forms, including banner ads, rich media, and more. It relies on visuals to convey its message.

- **Engagement Rate:** The metric that measures the level of engagement that a piece of content receives from an audience, often through likes, comments, shares, and interaction rates.

- **Geotargeting:** Delivering content to a user based on their geographic location. Particularly useful in mobile advertising and local business promotions.

- **Impressions:** The number of times an advertisement is displayed, regardless of whether it is clicked or not. It's a key metric for understanding an ad's reach.

- **Influencer Marketing:** Leveraging individuals with a strong online presence to promote products or services. Influencers can drive engagement and credibility.

- **Key Performance Indicator (KPI):** A measurable value that indicates how effectively a company is achieving its key business objectives, especially in advertising campaigns.

- **Landing Page:** A standalone web page created specifically for marketing or advertising campaigns, where visitors "land" after clicking on an ad. It's designed to drive a specific action.

- **Market Penetration:** The extent to which a product is recognized and bought by customers in a particular market. High market penetration indicates a strong market presence.

- **Media Buy:** The procurement of advertising space and time on various media channels, such as TV, radio, print, and online platforms.

- **Native Advertising:** A form of paid media where the ad experience follows the natural form and function of the user experience in which it is placed. Often seen in social media feeds and content websites.

- **Omnichannel Marketing:** A multi-channel approach that provides the customer with an integrated shopping experience. The customer can seamlessly switch between online and offline channels.

- **Organic Reach:** The number of people who see your content without paid distribution. Higher organic reach indicates strong content and high engagement from the audience.

- **Paid Search:** A form of pay-per-click advertising where advertisers pay a fee each time their ad is clicked, typically through search engines like Google.

- **Programmatic Advertising:** The use of automated systems and data analytics to buy advertising space in real-time, enabling highly targeted and efficient ad campaigns.

- **Reach:** The total number of different people or households exposed to an advertisement. It measures the spread of the message across the target audience.

- **Return on Investment (ROI):** The measure of the profitability of an ad campaign, calculated by dividing the net profit by the cost of the campaign. A high ROI indicates the campaign was successful.

- **Social Proof:** The psychological phenomenon where people assume the actions of others reflect the correct behavior for a given situation. Often used in testimonials and reviews to persuade potential consumers.

- **Split Testing:** Similar to A/B testing, it's the process of comparing multiple versions of a campaign element to see which one performs best.

- **Target Audience:** A specific group of people identified as the intended recipient of an advertisement or message. Tailoring ads to this group increases their effectiveness.

- **Unique Selling Proposition (USP):** A factor that differentiates a product from its competitors, such as quality, price, or novelty. Clearly communicating the USP is critical for effective advertising.

- **Viral Marketing:** A strategy that encourages individuals to share a marketing message with others, often leading to exponential growth in the message's visibility and effect.

This glossary provides just a glimpse into the rich lexicon of advertising. Mastering these terms can significantly enhance your ability to create impactful and persuasive marketing campaigns. Keep this glossary handy as a quick reference guide anytime you're crafting or analyzing ads. The more familiar you are with these terms, the more you'll be equipped to navigate the ever-evolving landscape of advertising.

## C: Further Reading and Resources

Advertising and marketing are fields that are constantly evolving, and staying ahead requires dedication to continuous learning. Within this section, you'll find a curated selection of books, articles, online courses, and other valuable resources that can further enhance your knowledge and skills in advertising. Whether you're looking to delve deeper into the psychology of consumer behavior or explore the latest trends in digital marketing, these resources will serve as a solid foundation for your ongoing education and professional development.

One of the most insightful books in understanding the underlying mechanisms of influence is **"Influence: The Psychology of Persuasion" by Robert Cialdini**. This book, a staple in the advertising world, explores the key principles that drive people to say "yes" and how you can apply these principles ethically in marketing campaigns. It's essential reading for anyone looking to master the art of persuasion.

For a more contemporary take on digital advertising and its metrics, you might consider **"Digital Marketing Analytics: Making Sense of Consumer Data in a Digital World" by Chuck Hemann and Ken Burbary**. This book provides comprehensive insights into how to interpret and utilize digital metrics effectively to refine and optimize your campaigns. It's particularly useful for those heavily involved in analytics and data-driven decision-making.

Additionally, dive into **"Building a StoryBrand: Clarify Your Message So Customers Will Listen" by Donald Miller**. This book stresses the importance of a clear and compelling message, helping you to craft stories that resonate with your audience. It's a practical guide for anyone looking to elevate their advertising messages by leveraging the power of storytelling.

An invaluable online resource for continuous upskilling is *Coursera*, which offers numerous courses across all areas of marketing and advertising. Specializations such as the *"Digital Marketing Specialization" by the University of Illinois* provide in-depth knowledge on topics like SEO, social media marketing, and content strategy. These courses are beneficial for both new learners and seasoned professionals wanting to refine their expertise.

Another robust platform is *LinkedIn Learning*, where industry experts provide lectures and workshops on a wide variety of topics.

Courses like *"SEO: Strategy and Techniques"* and *"Branding Foundations"* can help you stay updated with the latest trends and best practices. The subscription model allows access to a plethora of other business and technology-related courses, making it a worthwhile investment.

For those who like to keep their reading more concise and targeted, subscribing to industry-leading journals and blogs can be incredibly beneficial. Publications such as *Ad Age* and *Marketing Week* regularly feature cutting-edge articles on current trends, successful campaigns, and expert opinions. Blogs like *Moz* and *HubSpot* are excellent for staying informed about the latest advancements in digital marketing and SEO tactics.<

Attending conferences and seminars also offers fantastic opportunities for learning and networking. Events such as *Advertising Week* and *Content Marketing World* gather top industry professionals who share their insights and experiences. These events often present the latest research findings, innovative strategies, and case studies of successful marketing campaigns.

Furthermore, if you're someone who prefers a more structured learning approach, consider enrolling in formal education programs. Graduate programs like the *Master's in Integrated Marketing Communications* at Northwestern University or the *Master's in Digital Advertising* at the University of Texas at Austin are designed to provide comprehensive training and research opportunities in advanced marketing techniques.